THE WAY
MULTIMEDIA
WORKS

D1318669

SIMON COLLIN

Microsoft
PRESS

DK DIRECT

Series Editor: Robert Dinwiddie; **Series Art Editor:** Virginia Walter
Project Editor: Susan Schlachter
Art Editor: Sean Edwards; **Project Designer:** Nigel Coath
Production Manager: Ian Paton

MICROSOFT PRESS

Acquisitions Director: Dean Holmes; **Acquisitions Editor:** Lucinda Rowley
Project Editor: Katherine A. Krause; **Technical Director:** David Rygmyr

THE AUTHOR

Simon Collin is a journalist who has worked for *PC Magazine* and several other computer-related publications. He has been writing for seven years and has produced more than a dozen books on computers and computer-related topics.

ADDITIONAL CONTRIBUTORS

Illustrators: Anthony Bellue, Nigel Coath, Janos Marffy, Peter Serjeant; **Model Making:** Sean Edwards
Airbrushing: Janos Marffy, Roy Flooks; **Photography:** Tony Buckley, Andy Crawford, Steve Gorton
Technical Assistance: Stuart McEwan; **Typing Assistance:** Margaret Little

Library of Congress Cataloging-in-Publication Data

Collin, Simon.
   The way multimedia works / Simon Collin.
      p.   cm.
   Includes index.
   ISBN 1-55615-651-0
   1. Multimedia systems.   I. Title.
QA76.575.C65   1994
006.6—dc20   94-3424
                                                           CIP

Color Reproduction by Mullis Morgan, UK
Printed and Bound in the USA
123456789 QEQE 987654

Flexibook

CONTENTS

CHAPTER ONE

Introducing Multimedia

ome to the exciting world of media computing! In this chapter 'l find out what multimedia means, re some multimedia titles, and at the software you'll need to work multimedia applications.

CHAPTER TWO

Setting Up Your Multimedia PC

Learn about the hardware you'll need to equip your PC for multimedia — and how to install it.

CHAPTER THREE

Creating Multimedia with Windows

Find out about Windows' special utilities that can help you take control of your multimedia setup. You'll learn how to add sound and special effects to presentations and documents.

CHAPTER FOUR

Getting Adventurous

over how MIDI sound files, pic-, video sequences, and animation increase the appeal of your multi- a creations. A range of specialized are — such as paint packages and I sequencers — can help you create manipulate these various media.

CHAPTER FIVE

All Together Now

Learn how to plan and put together a multimedia presentation. This chapter looks at multimedia authoring packages and explains the steps you might follow to create a simple presentation using two different authoring programs.

REFERENCE

Reference Section

Turn to this section for some advice on common hardware and software problems, a listing of some additional software you might find useful, a review of copyright issues, and a glossary.

About This Book

Welcome to *The Way Multimedia Works*, the ultimate user-friendly guide to creating and running multimedia on your PC!

Multimedia is a term that seems to be on everyone's lips these days. This book is designed to make your introduction to the concept easy and fun. It includes full instructions on setting up a multimedia PC, shows you how to use Windows' own multimedia utilities, and provides practical advice about planning and putting together a simple multimedia presentation. You'll also find information about software that can help you with multimedia development.

ONE STEP AT A TIME

This book is organized so that you begin with the basics and move on to more advanced topics later. First you'll learn what multimedia is and explore a range of commercially available multimedia titles. Then you'll find out how to set yourself up with a multimedia PC — whether you want to upgrade an existing PC or buy an off-the-shelf multimedia machine. You'll find out about sound cards, CD-ROM drives, and the optimum monitor and video adapter for multimedia. As you move through the book, you'll find plenty of step-by-step advice on a range of multimedia tasks, such as recording and editing sound files, creating animation, and capturing video sequences.

THE WYSIWYG CONCEPT

By the way, I'm the WYSIWYG wizard, and you'll find me popping up quite often in this book, handing out a few tips on getting the most from your multimedia PC.

One of the first questions you may be asking is: What does the term WYSIWYG have to do with it? Well, WYSIWYG stands for "What You See Is What You Get." It was coined some years ago to describe programs with a special feature — namely that *what you see* on the screen is the same as *what you get* when you print it out. In this book we'll be turning the WYSIWYG concept around a little bit.

Throughout the book, you'll find practical instructions for using various types of software — including not only the multimedia utilities that come with Windows, but also some specialized packages, such as image editing and video capture software and multimedia authoring tools. In each case, the instructions are

The World of MIDI
Learn about MIDI devices — and how to record and play MIDI music on your PC — on pages 70 to 77.

Using Windows' Multimedia Utilities
Find out about Windows' multimedia utilities, such as Sound Recorder, Object Packager, and Media Player, on pages 54 to 67.

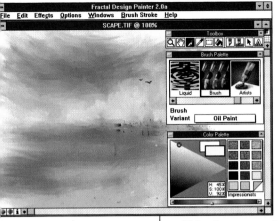

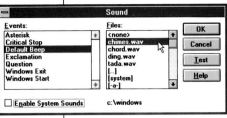

accompanied by visual prompts showing what you would see on your monitor when you use the software. In other words, *what you see* on the page is the same as *what you get* on the screen.

SCREENS AND FRAGMENTS

Sometimes you'll see a screen shot (like the one shown above left) that illustrates how the whole screen will look at a particular stage in an operation. Or you might see a dialog box (like the one shown above right) or a series of screen "fragments" (like those shown at right) to help you follow step-by-step instructions.

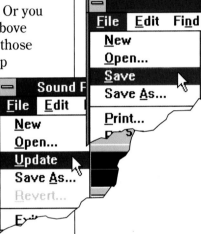

TIPS AND WARNINGS

In addition to the insights I'll provide, you'll see various tips in colored boxes scattered throughout the book. The *pink* boxes contain warnings about some common pitfalls you may run into when using multimedia hardware and software, and they offer advice on what to do when things go wrong. The *green* boxes provide answers to some common questions about multimedia.

A Hazard to Floppies!
Inside your loudspeakers are magnets. If you place a floppy disk too close to a speaker while it is working, you might accidentally erase what's on your disk. Keep floppy disks several inches away from speakers.

Play Audio Tracks?
If you want to use Media Player to play a particular track on an audio CD, choose *Tracks* from Media Player's *Scale* menu. The scale is then divided into tracks instead of time units. Scroll to the track you want to hear and click on the Play button.

REFERENCE SECTION

At the back of the book, you'll find a Reference Section. This includes important information, such as copyright issues you should be aware of; a listing of some useful software packages to help you develop your own multimedia; and a section on troubleshooting some of the problems that you might encounter with your multimedia hardware or software. You'll also find a short glossary of multimedia terms and a comprehensive index. As you read through the book, you'll see a number of technical terms that have been italicized — these are all defined in the glossary.

EASY READING

The only way to become comfortable with any new computing concept is to get hands-on experience. We believe that *The Way Multimedia Works* is the easiest, most practical, and most enjoyable way for you to get that experience. Read on!

5

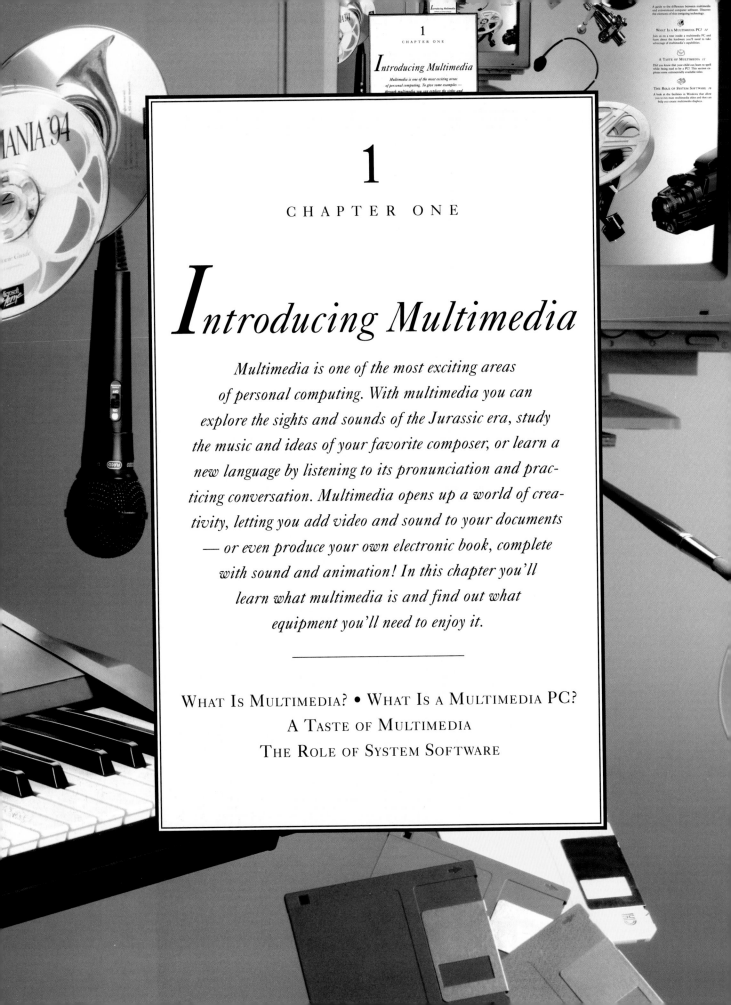

1

CHAPTER ONE

Introducing Multimedia

Multimedia is one of the most exciting areas of personal computing. With multimedia you can explore the sights and sounds of the Jurassic era, study the music and ideas of your favorite composer, or learn a new language by listening to its pronunciation and practicing conversation. Multimedia opens up a world of creativity, letting you add video and sound to your documents — or even produce your own electronic book, complete with sound and animation! In this chapter you'll learn what multimedia is and find out what equipment you'll need to enjoy it.

WHAT IS MULTIMEDIA? • WHAT IS A MULTIMEDIA PC?
A TASTE OF MULTIMEDIA
THE ROLE OF SYSTEM SOFTWARE

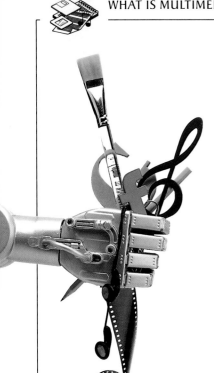

What Is Multimedia?

MULTIMEDIA COMPUTING MEANS DIFFERENT THINGS to different people. To some, it is the thrill of computer games; to others, it is a source of reference for any topic under (and beyond!) the sun. The combination of different media such as sound and vision, all controlled with a personal computer, has opened up a new world of education and entertainment.

From Mono to Multi...

The first PCs were monomedia. They could not play sounds and they displayed only text on their screens. But over the last 10 years, a number of new technologies have emerged that have extended the power and scope of the personal computer — faster chips, sound cards, bigger monitors, and so on. Gradually, a platform for multimedia has emerged.

The first multimedia software consisted mainly of games. Then compact disc technology was developed, and the CD's massive storage capacity encouraged a flood of educational and reference titles on *CD-ROM* (read-only memory) discs. Today the multiple media can include text, pictures, audio, animation, and video clips. Here's an example from *The Software Toolworks Multimedia Encyclopedia*:

Video
Click on the Video icon to activate a new window where you can watch a clip of an eagle fishing.

Sound
Click on the Sound icon and a small window will appear. Click on the Play button to hear the sound of a bald eagle.

Graphics
Click on the Picture icon to see drawings of the golden eagle and the bald eagle.

Text
Drop down the Outline box to see a summary of the article displayed in the main window. Click on an item in the box to move quickly to that item in the text.

The Software Toolworks Multimedia Encyclopedia - [eagle]

File   Edit   Search   Text   Window   Bookmark   Help

eagle

Eagles are large predatory birds that have been symbols of power, courage, and immortality since ancient times. The more than 50 species all belong to the HAWK family, Accipitridae, order Falconiformes. Eagles inhabit all major land regions except Antarctica and New Zealand. Although once abundant, some eagles are becoming rare and face extinction. One rare species is the bald eagle, Haliaeetus leucocephalus, the national emblem of the United States. Although protected by law, some large eagles are killed by farmers and gamekeepers or captured for use in falconry. In addition, the bald eagle, like other birds, has been affected by the widespread use of pesticides that, ingested, can weaken eggs.

Appearance

Eagles are noted for their strength and keen vision. Most eagles range from 60 to 90 cm [2 to 3 ft] long and have wingspans of about 180 cm [6 ft]; one of the smallest, however, the Ayres' eagle, Hieraetus dubius, is only 40 cm [16 in] long, and the largest, the harpy eagle, Harpia harpyja, reaches 100 cm [39 in] in length and has a wingspan up to 2.4 m [8 ft].

All eagles have large, heavy, hooked bills and strong, sharp claws called talons. They

Use cursor keys or scroll bar to scroll article, select icons for features   Page 1 of 4

INTERACTIVE MULTIMEDIA

Some multimedia programs are *linear* — a sort of slide show on a computer screen, in which user involvement is limited to advancing to the next information screen or going back to view the previous one.

Others programs are *interactive*. Interactive multimedia puts you in control and lets you steer freely through the labyrinth of images, sound, and video clips in a program. Clicking on a predefined area known as a *hotspot* will display another file in the program; the linked file can consist of an image, a sound file, a video clip, or a window filled with new information.

Good Connections
Most commercial multi-media titles let the user control the flow of action. By clicking on certain buttons or other screen areas (hotspots), users can follow whatever path of inquiry takes their interest, or they can go back to their original screen at any time. The example on this page comes from Microsoft Dinosaurs.

How Does It Work?
When you click on a picture or button, the software looks to see if it links to other files: a button might link to a new page or play a sound file for instance. These software links between images, sounds, and commands are called *hypermedia,* and they control how an interactive multimedia presentation works.

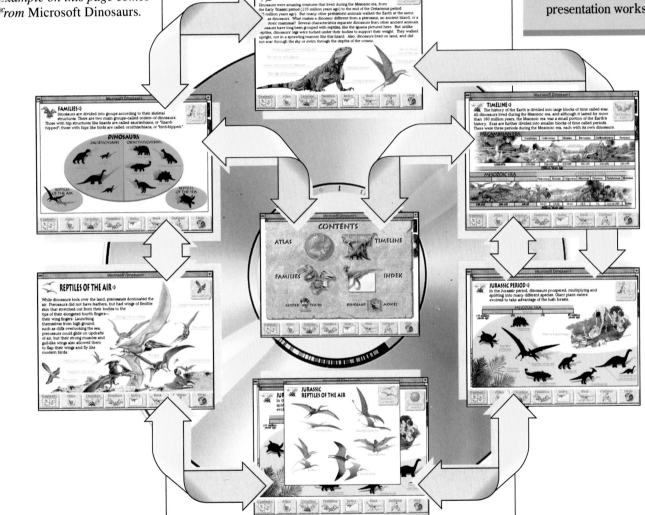

A number of methods are used to indicate hotspots in multimedia titles (see left). Sometimes the cursor changes to a hand when it is positioned at a hotspot. Hotspots in the text are often shown through the use of colors, underlining, or capital letters.

What Is a Multimedia PC?

BEFORE YOU CAN HAVE FUN WITH MULTIMEDIA, you must have a PC that can handle audio and video. These days, many PCs come with the necessary elements already installed. If you're not in the market for a new machine, however, you will have to upgrade your existing system. You can do this either by buying the separate components individually or by purchasing an upgrade kit (see page 42).

The first purchases you should make are a *sound card* and a pair of speakers. Although a PC comes with a built-in speaker, this emits little more than beeps. A sound card and speakers will make your PC sing.

Your next purchase should be a *CD-ROM drive*. A CD-ROM drive is not an essential part of a multimedia PC, but many of the multimedia titles available in stores come on CD-ROM discs. A CD-ROM disc can hold over 600 times as much information as a floppy disk, and this vast quantity of storage space opens up a world of entertainment, education, and reference (see pages 12 to 15 and page 120 for a glimpse of the multimedia titles available on CD-ROM).

Memory
A multimedia PC needs a lot of memory because it has to move a lot of data around very quickly. Be sure that your machine has 4 megabytes (MB) of RAM at the very least. If your PC has 8 MB or more of RAM, your software will work much faster and more smoothly.

Sound Card
The sound card fits into an expansion connector inside your PC and lets you record or play sound (see pages 20 to 31 for more on sound cards).

Speakers
You'll need a pair of speakers to hear the sounds you play on your PC. Don't attach the speakers to the sides of your monitor — the magnetic coils in them can damage your monitor screen.

PC Speaker
All PCs come with a built-in speaker; a sound card will all but replace it for your system's sounds.

Microphone
You'll need a microphone if you want to record your own sounds.

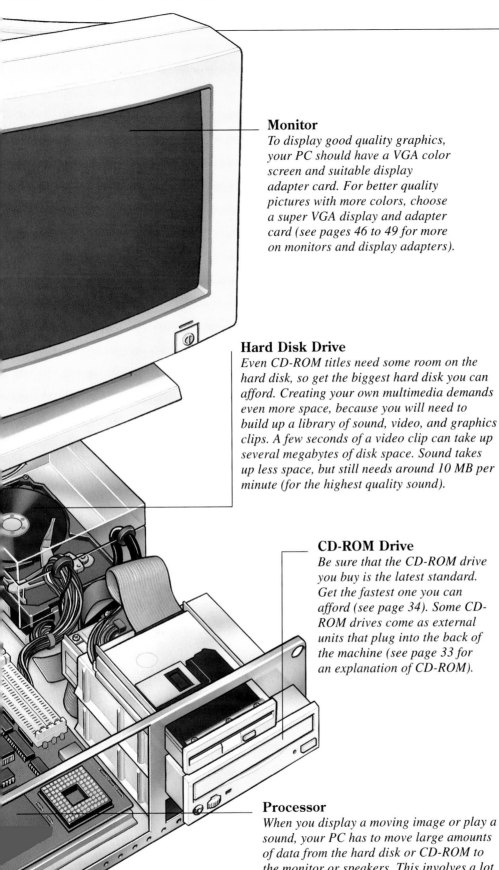

Monitor
To display good quality graphics, your PC should have a VGA color screen and suitable display adapter card. For better quality pictures with more colors, choose a super VGA display and adapter card (see pages 46 to 49 for more on monitors and display adapters).

Hard Disk Drive
Even CD-ROM titles need some room on the hard disk, so get the biggest hard disk you can afford. Creating your own multimedia demands even more space, because you will need to build up a library of sound, video, and graphics clips. A few seconds of a video clip can take up several megabytes of disk space. Sound takes up less space, but still needs around 10 MB per minute (for the highest quality sound).

CD-ROM Drive
Be sure that the CD-ROM drive you buy is the latest standard. Get the fastest one you can afford (see page 34). Some CD-ROM drives come as external units that plug into the back of the machine (see page 33 for an explanation of CD-ROM).

Processor
When you display a moving image or play a sound, your PC has to move large amounts of data from the hard disk or CD-ROM to the monitor or speakers. This involves a lot of processing, so a fast, powerful central processing unit (CPU), such as the 80486 or Pentium processor, is highly desirable.

Buying Power!
Although technically you can run multimedia titles on a PC that has an 80386 microprocessor, a minimum of 2 MB of RAM, and a 30 MB hard disk, a more powerful system will give you much more enjoyment. You'll do best to spend your money on a lot of memory and a big hard disk, especially if you want to experiment with creating your own multimedia projects. Graphics, sound, and video clips take up large amounts of disk space.

Out of Space?
You can easily double the capacity of your hard disk by using a disk compression program. This compresses files and lets you store twice as much data as an uncompressed hard disk.

A Taste of Multimedia

N̲ow that you know what you need to run multimedia, let's take a more detailed look at what you can do with it. You have already been introduced to some commercial software titles; over the next few pages you will learn a little more about the huge selection of titles available. More titles are featured on page 120 of the Reference Section.

Off-the-Shelf Titles

When you shop for a multimedia title, remember that CD-ROM does not necessarily equal multimedia. CD-ROM discs are useful for titles that need huge data storage capacities, and some discs consist of nothing but text and numbers.

Remember also that some multimedia titles come on floppy disks as well as on CD-ROM. Games and adventure programs, especially, are often available on both CD-ROM and floppy disks.

Multimedia titles range from games that use real-life video to create another world to educational titles that help you learn a new language. Whichever you choose, you will be amazed at the feast of color and sound they offer. Here we showcase some of the features in a selection of popular titles.

Wordy Titles
Some CD-ROM titles are simply textbooks in electronic form. Other "data buckets" include telephone directories and tables of financial information.

Microsoft Encarta

Instant Interaction
Each icon on the opening screen (above) is a hotspot with its own search technique. Position the cursor on an icon to see where it will take you (below).

Microsoft's CD-ROM encyclopedia, *Encarta*, uses text, pictures, animation, video, and sound to provide a wealth of information on almost any subject you can think of.
The opening screen offers several different navigation techniques. To get back to the article you viewed the last time you used *Encarta*, you can click on the *Enter Encarta* button at the bottom of the window. Otherwise, you enter the title by clicking on one of the icons.

To look up something specific, you can click on *Contents* for the index and then type in the name of the topic you want to investigate. To examine a particular theme, you can click on *Category Browser* and then select an area of interest from the category list.

The *Gallery Wizard* helps you locate pictures, video, maps, and sound, while the *Find Wizard* lets you stipulate certain criteria for your search — for instance, a specific period of history.

Search Options
You can type names into the Contents *box (above), or search for a topic by category (below).*

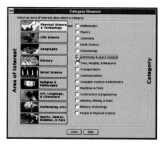

THE MAIN WINDOW

However you access a topic from the opening screen, the main window (below) will appear. Here you can read about your chosen topic and make use of a number of tools to explore the subject further.

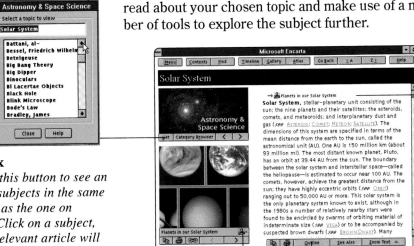

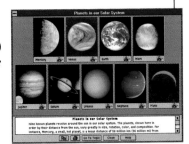

Article Frame
This part of the main window contains the text describing the topic. Colored, underlined text indicates a hotspot; click on a hotspot to see the entry for that subject.

List Box
Click on this button to see an index of subjects in the same category as the one on display. Click on a subject, and the relevant article will appear in a new window.

Gallery Items
The Gallery Frame (bottom left of screen) is a quick guide to the image and sound items in each entry. Click on the icon to expand an image or play a sound file.

Print and Copy
The Copy button on the left lets you copy text from the article to the Windows clipboard. The Print button lets you print out the article in the main window.

Outline Box
This box gives quick access to information in the article frame. Image and sound icons (like those on the right) indicate gallery items.

THE BUTTON BAR

At the top of each main window is the button bar. From here, you can access the *Contents* box, go back to windows you viewed previously, locate images and sounds, find your way in time, and even explore the world.

Gallery
The Gallery button opens the Gallery Browser box, where you can hear and view all the sound and image files in Encarta. Clicking on the Slide Show button takes you through these files automatically.

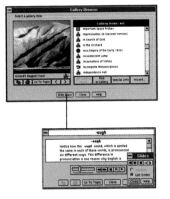

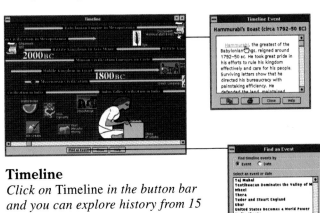

Timeline
Click on Timeline in the button bar and you can explore history from 15 million BC to the present. Hotspots offer plenty to read about — people, events, civilizations, and customs. Click on Find an Event for easy entry to a specific point in history (right).

Atlas
Clicking on Atlas in the main button bar brings up the Atlas. The Atlas contains maps and information from countries around the world. Unusual pronunciations can be clarified with a click on a sound icon.

Musical Instruments

Many of the multimedia reference titles available on CD-ROM disc concentrate on specialized topics. *Microsoft Musical Instruments*, for example, is a guide to over 200 instruments, both well known and obscure. Each instrument is explained in detail, and the text is accompanied by photographs and sound samples. You can even play the notes of some instruments yourself!

SEARCH TECHNIQUES

The *Contents* screen helps you find your way around by grouping the contents under three main headings — *Families of Instruments, Musical Ensembles*, and *Instruments of the World*. An index provides quick access to specific instruments. If you click on *Families of Instruments*, for example, a new screen will show your options for further investigation. Clicking on *Strings* lets you see the instruments that constitute the string family.

Once you select a specific instrument, the screen comes alive with hotspots and icons. The *Play* icon contains a musical interlude demonstrating the instrument's sound. Clicking on the *Sound Box* icon lets you play each note yourself or hear the different effects the instrument can create. A *Facts Box* provides additional background information on the instrument.

The Opening Screen
The opening screen offers an index and three other options for getting information.

Exploration Paths
Choose from one of the above search techniques, or access a topic directly via the index.

A Family of Strings
Choose one of the families and you can then zoom in on a specific instrument.

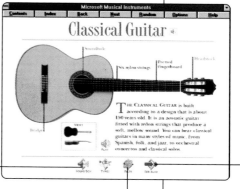

Get Specific
The main screen for the classical guitar.

The Sound Box
Play each separate note and hear a selection of styles.

Microsoft Musical Instruments contains over 1,500 sound files and around 500 photographs. It caters to all musical tastes and lets you listen to music from every point on the globe.

See Also
A good way to explore further.

The Facts Box
Everything you want to know about the origin and development of the instrument.

Just Grandma and Me

The children's story *Just Grandma and Me*, published by Broderbund Software, is narrated by the main character, Little Critter. He tells what happened to him during a day at the beach with his grandma, and each little adventure is accompanied by animated graphics. Users can have the tale read to them or can play interactively with the title.

The Opening Screen
Children can use the title interactively, or simply listen to the story being read to them.

FUN AND EDUCATIONAL

By choosing the *Let Me Play* option children can turn pages when they want to. They can also click on different parts of the screen to initiate animated sequences.

These sequences are all accompanied by sound effects. Click on the lifeguard, for instance, and he will blow his whistle. Click on Grandma and she will speak and make gestures. Each element on the page comes alive with a click of the mouse. You can see some of the animated sequences below.

Help with Reading
Words are highlighted as they are narrated. Users can also click on individual words to hear how they are pronounced.

Clicking on the seagull causes the bird to jump up and down.

Click on the pier and a pelican appears. The bird then uses a captive fish to entice another fish into its beak.

Even the empty sea holds a surprise — click on it and a yacht sails across the screen.

One click on the pufferfish and it blows up to five times its previous size.

When prompted, the crab performs an undersea dance and then catches a fish in its claws.

Click on Little Critter's diving mask and a large fish swims up, plants a kiss on the glass, and retreats giggling.

The program does more than simply entertain children; it improves reading skills by highlighting words as Little Critter reads them. Users can also click on individual words to hear them read aloud.

The Role of System Software

THE MULTIMEDIA DEVICES IN YOUR PC, like the sound card and CD-ROM drive, need complex instructions to control them. The CD-ROM drive has to be told when to play the disc loaded in it, and what particular parts to play at any one time. To play a sound, the PC needs to know how to access the sound card and the sound to be played needs to be transferred from storage to the speakers. It's the job of the system software to carry out all this behind-the-scenes work. For most multimedia applications, the system software used is Microsoft Windows.

The Multimedia Extensions

Windows, together with MS-DOS, provides the link between your system hardware and the software that you run on your PC. When version 3.1 of Windows came out, these links were extended to include those for controlling multimedia hardware. Windows 3.1 contains everything you need to run most multimedia titles and create your own multimedia displays — if you have the appropriate multimedia equipment installed.

When you install Windows 3.1 on your PC, the multimedia extensions are automatically installed at the same time. You can see most of them in the *Accessories* window, though some are contained in the *Control Panel* window. Double-click on the *Accessories* group icon in Program Manager and you'll see three items that support multimedia: *Media Player, Sound Recorder,* and *Object Packager*.

Setting Standards

Multimedia PCs are more complicated than ordinary PCs, with more hardware devices that must work together, and more types of data to understand. By providing a set way of linking multimedia hardware and software, the multimedia extensions let manufacturers design products that they know will be compatible with each other.

I Only Have Windows 3.0!

If you have not yet upgraded to Windows 3.1, the multimedia extensions are a good reason for doing so. Otherwise you can buy a Multimedia Extensions pack, which will add multimedia capabilities to version 3.0 of Windows.

Media Player

Media Player *is used to play multimedia files, like animation and sound files. You can also use it to play CD audio discs in a CD-ROM drive.*

Object Packager

This is used to embed "objects" like sound or video files into a document.

Sound Recorder

Sound Recorder *lets you record, play, pause, stop, fast-forward, or rewind a sound. You can also use it to add special effects, such as an echo.*

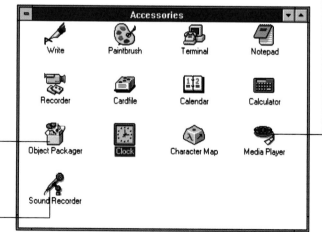

Now open the *Control Panel* window. Here you'll see the *Sound* and *Drivers* extensions. If your hardware supports MIDI, you'll also see the *MIDI Mapper* icon.

MIDI Mapper
This complex tool is used for specifying music channels; your PC must have special MIDI hardware to use it. Most multimedia PCs do not.

The Sound Extension
This is used to assign sounds to different system events. For instance, you can set it up to play a certain sound whenever you launch a program.

The Drivers Extension
When you install a new hardware device, like a CD-ROM drive, you may need to use this extension to install the software that Windows uses to "drive" the device (see page 29 for an explanation of drivers).

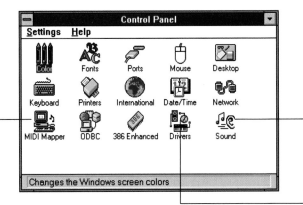

Making Your Own Multimedia

Windows 3.1 can also be used to create simple multimedia projects. Whether you want to enliven business presentations or simply produce a project for your own amusement, adding multimedia elements to familiar software like word processing programs is fun and easy. More complex projects, such as creating an interactive multimedia title,

need special multimedia programming tools called *authoring software* (for more on authoring tools, see page 100). Whatever method you choose to create multimedia, a range of software is available to help you with specific elements of the project. We will cover these elements in more detail later, but for now here's a sampler of what's available:

Images
You can create your own images using a paint program, or you can import photographs and pre-drawn pictures from a variety of sources. Special effects can be added to these images with the aid of retouching software. (For more information on image software, see pages 80 to 85.)

Video
If you have a *video capture* card and have saved a still image or video sequence to your hard disk, you can edit the images, add special effects, and play the sequence. Best of all, you can play the image or sequence on any PC — it doesn't need any special hardware. (For more information on capturing video, see pages 86 to 91.)

Animation
Animation looks good and is fun to create. You can make your own animation using a paint package to draw each picture, or "cel", and then use animation software to turn it into a moving cartoon. (For more information on animation software, see pages 94 to 97.)

Sound
Sound livens up multimedia presentations. You can record stereo sound if you have a sound card, and a range of software lets you edit sound. (For more information on sound in multimedia, see pages 20 to 31, 52 to 61, and 70 to 77.)

2

CHAPTER TWO

Setting Up Your Multimedia PC

*You've seen a little of what can be
done with multimedia. In this chapter, you'll
learn how to equip your own PC for multimedia. To
get started, you'll need a sound card and (optionally)
a CD-ROM drive; you might also need to check out the
suitability of your monitor and display adapter card.
This chapter describes all these hardware items in
detail — how they work, what they do, and
how you can configure each component
to get the best performance.*

SOUND CARDS • CD-ROM DRIVES
UPGRADE KITS • PERFORMANCE UPGRADES
MONITORS AND DISPLAY

SOUND CARDS *20*

Once you've installed a sound card and connected it to some speakers, your computer can start playing high-quality stereo sound. You can also use your sound card as a sophisticated tape recorder, capable of storing sounds, voices, or music on your hard disk.

CD-ROM DRIVES *32*

Most multimedia PCs have a CD-ROM drive. Learn how CD-ROM works, how to choose from the different CD-ROM drive standards, and how to install a drive in your PC.

UPGRADE KITS *42*

A convenient way of upgrading your existing PC to a multimedia PC is to buy an all-in-one upgrade kit. Here are some of the main points to think about when purchasing a kit.

PERFORMANCE UPGRADES *44*

Some advice on upgrading other parts of your PC's hardware, such as your computer's RAM and hard disk, to cope with the demands of multimedia.

MONITORS AND DISPLAY *46*

There's no point to any multimedia presentation if the images can't be clearly seen — so you need to make sure your monitor is up to par and configured correctly. If you're confused about pixels, resolution, display modes, and color depth, you'll find the answers here.

Sound Cards

What About the PC Speaker?

All PCs are fitted with a small loudspeaker mounted inside the case. It's connected to an electronic component that can make simple noises — warning beeps and squeaks. With a little tinkering, you can get this loudspeaker to play simple music or sound effects. However, the sounds you can generate are limited, and there's no feature to let you record sounds. That's why, if you want to really enjoy multimedia, you'll need a sound card.

A SOUND CARD HAS TWO BASIC PURPOSES. First, it can take sound signals — either picked up by a microphone or generated by an electronic instrument — and convert these into a stream of numbers for storage as a file on a computer disk. Second, it can take sound files and play these through speakers, headphones, or an electronic musical instrument. A sound card can play sounds or notes in stereo and produces high-quality sound — generally as good as the CD player in your stereo system.

Sound Card

A sound card is a rigid fiberglass card, bristling with electronic components. You install it by plugging it into a free expansion slot in your PC's system unit. At the back of the card are a number of ports and sockets for connecting the card to a microphone, speakers, headphones, and electronic musical instruments.

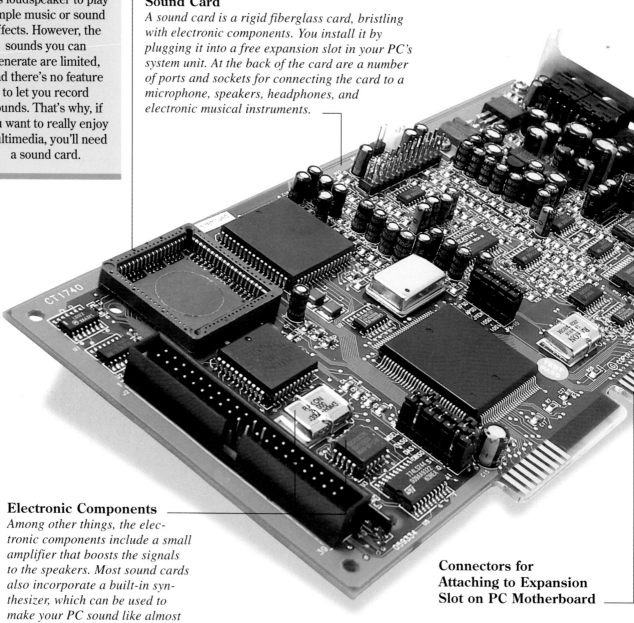

Electronic Components

Among other things, the electronic components include a small amplifier that boosts the signals to the speakers. Most sound cards also incorporate a built-in synthesizer, which can be used to make your PC sound like almost any musical instrument.

Connectors for Attaching to Expansion Slot on PC Motherboard

Microphone

With a microphone plugged into the sound card, you can record any sound — your voice, a special effect, a musical instrument, or a symphony orchestra. The sound card turns these sounds into electrical signals and stores them on your PC's hard disk as sound files. Many cards come with a microphone, but if you don't have one, see page 26 to find out about the basic types of microphones.

Speakers

To make a sound, the sound card reads the data in a file stored on your hard disk (or a CD-ROM) and turns the numbers back into sound. But you'll only hear the sound if you plug a pair of speakers (or headphones) into the sound card. Some cards let you connect your PC into your stereo system so that you can use its amplifier and more powerful speakers.

What's a Sound File?

A sound file is just like any other file on your computer's hard disk. The main thing you'll want to do with a sound file is, of course, listen to it by using your sound card to play it through some speakers. But you can also copy a file, move it to a floppy disk, rename it, or, if you get bored with the sound, delete it.

Joystick

Some sound cards have a joystick port — this port may also serve as the MIDI port (with the use of an adapter, both the joystick and MIDI device can be run from the same port). A joystick is essential to control many games. Some PCs already have a joystick port. If the sound card has one too, there's no problem. The two joystick ports can work together.

MIDI Device

Some sound cards have a connector called a MIDI port. This allows the sound card to communicate with a variety of electronic musical instruments (MIDI devices). You can plug MIDI-compatible synthesizer keyboards, drum machines, or electronic guitars into your PC and then use your PC to record the notes played on them or control the notes they play.

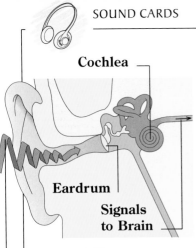

Cochlea

Eardrum

Signals
to Brain

Sound Wave

The Human Ear
You can hear a sound because of a small pressure detector, the eardrum, deep inside your ear. As sound waves hit the eardrum, it vibrates. The vibrations are transmitted via tiny bones to a hearing organ, the cochlea. The cochlea converts the vibrations into signals that are sent via a nerve to your brain.

How a Sound Card Works

When you set out to buy a sound card, you will probably be most interested in the quality of the sound produced — but later, you may want to use a card for other purposes, such as recording music. Before you make a buying decision, you'll find it useful to know a little about how a sound card works. This will help you understand the differences between different cards.

SOUNDS AND NUMBERS
Computers are not intrinsically adept at handling sounds. A sound is actually a continuously varying pressure wave in the air, whereas a PC can handle information only in the form of binary numbers (strings of 1s and 0s) — i.e., discrete chunks of data rather than continuously varying information.

The basic job of a sound card is to convert sounds into series of binary numbers and vice-versa. These numbers are stored in the computer as *sound files*. A sound card can create and play two different types of sound files — *waveform files* and *MIDI files* (nonwaveform files). The important differences between them are listed on the next page. Here we'll concentrate mainly on waveform files.

Choose Carefully!
One important consideration when buying a sound card is to check whether it offers a built-in CD-ROM interface — this can be very useful if you are thinking of installing a CD-ROM drive later on. Ideally, the connector should be a SCSI interface — see page 36 for further information.

Recording Waveform Files
A PC with a microphone and sound card works a lot like your ear does. The microphone turns sound waves into a continuously varying electrical signal called an *analog signal*. At fixed time intervals, the sound card records the strength of this signal as a digit. The sound card repeats the operation, which is called *sampling*, thousands of times every second. The process is called *analog to digital conversion*.

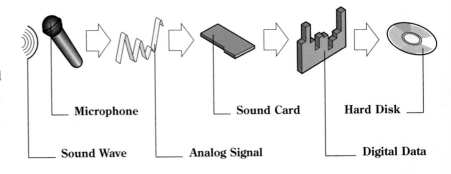

Microphone

Sound Wave

Sound Card

Analog Signal

Hard Disk

Digital Data

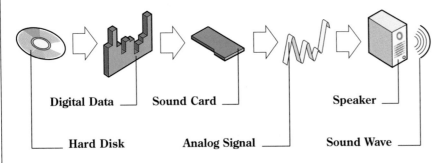

Digital Data

Sound Card

Analog Signal

Hard Disk

Speaker

Sound Wave

Producing Sound
To produce sound, the sound card does exactly the opposite of analog to digital conversion — it converts the stream of digits stored as a sound file in the computer into an analog signal that powers loudspeakers. The sound card varies the strength of the signal according to the sizes of the numbers in the sound file. The process is called *digital to analog conversion*.

Types of Sound Files

As you explore multimedia, you'll come across two kinds of sound files.

Waveform Files

■ These files store information about sound waves and are produced by the process called sampling.

■ Any type of sound — voices, music, and special effects — can be stored as a waveform file.

■ The files usually have the file extension WAV.

■ Because of the amount of data stored, waveform files are often large.

■ When you play a waveform file, you hear the same sound no matter what equipment you use.

MIDI Files

■ Files of this sort store instructions for making sounds, rather than sounds themselves.

■ They can be used to store only music.

■ MIDI files usually have the file extension MID.

■ MIDI files are more compact than waveform files.

■ A MIDI file can generate sounds only by being fed into a synthesizer — either a special chip on your sound card or an external synthesizer.

■ The notes in a MIDI file can be played to sound like different musical instruments.

SAMPLING RATES

A waveform file is produced by breaking a sound wave into tiny pieces and storing each piece as a small, digital sample of the sound — a process known as sampling. When a sound is being recorded as a waveform file, the more samples that can be taken every second, the more accurately the shape of the sound wave will be represented in the computer — and, in turn, the more accurately the original signal will be reproduced when it is played.

The number of samples taken per second is called the *sampling rate*. If you take ten samples of a sound each second, you won't even be able to recognize the original sound when it's played — you'll hear a series of tones. To get a reasonably accurate representation of a sound, a sound card needs to take several thousand samples every second.

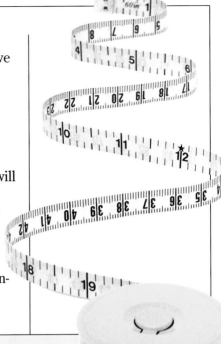

Sound Wave Sampling

Illustrated below is a comparison of the effects of recording — at two different sampling rates — a few thousandths of a second of a sound wave produced by a musical instrument, and then playing the sound back.

Digitized Wave

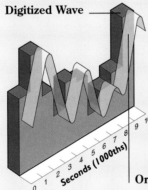

Seconds (1000ths)

Original Wave

Sampling at 1,000 Times per Second (1 kHz)

Here the sound wave has been sampled at the relatively low rate of 1,000 times per second — or one *kilohertz (kHz)*.

When the digitized waveform is reconstructed for playback, it differs markedly from the original wave — so it will not accurately reproduce its sound.

Wave Reconstructed for Playback

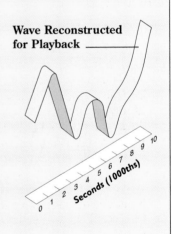

Seconds (1000ths)

Digitized Wave

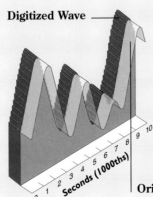

Seconds (1000ths)

Original Wave

Sampling at 11,000 Times per Second (11 kHz)

Here the sound has been sampled at a rate of 11 kHz — the lowest sampling rate of most sound cards. When the digitally encoded waveform is reconstructed, it provides a much more accurate (though not perfect) representation of the original waveform.

Wave Reconstructed for Playback

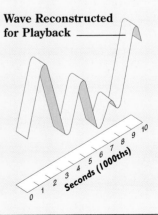

Seconds (1000ths)

STANDARD SAMPLING RATES

Most sound cards let you adjust the sampling rate. The lowest sampling rate of most sound cards is 11,000 samples per second (11 kHz). You will get a higher quality recording by choosing a sampling rate of 22,000 times per second (22 kHz). Some more expensive cards can manage a sampling rate of 44 kHz (44,000 times every second). These give the best quality sound recordings.

A high sampling rate is particularly important for high-fidelity recording and playing of music. It is less vital for recording and playing voices.

MORE BITS, BETTER QUALITY

There is another factor that affects sound quality — the number of computer bits available to store each sound sample. When the sound card measures the *amplitude* (strength) of a sound wave, the precision of the measurement depends on the range of values available. In 4-bit sound cards, only 4 bits are used per sample, and with 4 bits only 16 different values are available. If the original waveform has a lot of fine detail, much of this will be lost, because there will be enough values to represent only the broad shape of the waveform.

To solve this problem, the sound card needs to use more bits to store each sound sample in order to provide more possible values. An 8-bit sound card provides 256 measurement values, and a 16-bit card provides 65,536 different values. For the highest fidelity recording and production of sound, a 16-bit card is preferable.

Digital Delights

Ideally, you should not hear any difference between a sound recorded by your PC and then played through speakers and the original sound. A 16-bit sound card uses the same number of bits as the CD player in your stereo. So it will produce sound of exactly the same quality.

Why 16-Bit Sound Is Better

The *bit* is the most basic unit for information storage on a computer. Think of a bit as a switch that can either be flipped up (representing 1) or flipped down (representing 0).

8 Bits

With a group of 8 bits (a byte), there are 256 (2^8) different combinations in which the switches can be flipped up or down — so 8 bits can be used to store any number from 0 to 255.

16 Bits

With 16 bits (two bytes), there are 65,536 (2^{16}) possible ways in which the switches can be arranged — so 16 bits can be used to store any number from 0 to 65,535. That's why 16-bit sampling of sounds is so much more precise.

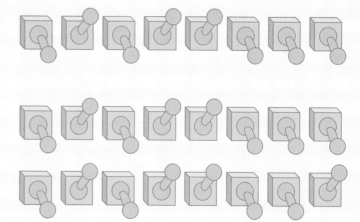

Do I Need a MIDI Port?

You'll need a MIDI port on your sound card only if you want to connect your sound card to an electronic instrument such as a keyboard synthesizer or a drum machine. If you don't have a MIDI port, you won't be able to use your PC to record from or play music through these instruments. However, you can still listen to MIDI sound files, provided the sound card has a built-in synthesizer.

There's an important difference between the speaker port and the MIDI port. A speaker port carries actual sound signals. A MIDI port carries instructions to electronic instruments to play sounds — instructions such as "Play Middle C" or "Release Middle C." So to make music using MIDI, you rely on the soundmaking abilities of other instruments. You'll find out more about MIDI on pages 70 through 77.

Sounds Take Up Space!
The higher the quality of the sound, the more disk space the sound will take up. A sound recorded on an 8-bit card at 11 kHz takes around 11 KB of disk space for each second of sound. Record with a 16-bit card at a sampling rate of 22 kHz, and you will use up 44 KB of disk space for each second of sound — or around 2.6 MB for a whole minute! If you record in stereo, it will double the disk space again.

Which Sound Card for Me?

Many different sound cards are available. Cards such as those in the Sound Blaster and the Pro Audio series can record all types of sounds as waveform files and can play good quality sounds. These cards use an FM synthesizer for playing MIDI files (see "What Is an FM Synthesizer?" at left). Cards such as the Turtle Beach MultiSound card have a higher-end synthesizer but are more expensive. If you see a sound card with the MPC (Multimedia PC Council) logo, it means that the card can do most basic multimedia tasks: it has good sound quality, a synthesizer, a MIDI port, a joystick port, and a CD-ROM interface, so it's a safe bet.

Bear the following points in mind when buying a sound card for your system:

■ A 16-bit card provides more accurate sound than an 8-bit card, but it also is a more expensive card. Similarly, a card offering sampling at 22 kHz or 44 kHz is more expensive than one offering only 11 kHz.

■ If you want to record and play voices only, and are not too concerned about quality, an 8-bit sound card with a sampling rate of 11 kHz will suffice.

■ If you want to make high-fidelity recordings of music or sound effects — and get high quality playback — you should use a 16-bit sound card with a 22-kHz or 44-kHz sampling rate. However, you'll need a large, fast hard disk to handle the sound files you'll create.

■ Make sure the card has a MIDI port if you wish to control or record from electronic musical instruments.

What Is an FM Synthesizer?
A synthesizer is a device that creates sounds. There are two main types. FM synthesizers, which are used on many popular sound cards, create different sounds by changing the frequency of a basic signal so that it matches the desired sound as closely as possible. Other synthesizers work by playing back stored recorded samples of real instruments or made-up sounds. Sound cards that use the latter method tend to cost more than the FM-synthesis cards.

Buying Speakers and a Microphone

You'll need a microphone if you want to record voices, music, or other sounds as waveform sound files, and you'll need speakers for hearing sound files, regardless of whether you or someone else has recorded them. It's worth choosing these items carefully, since they will determine the quality of the sound you hear almost as much as the sound card itself.

Unidirectional Microphone

MICROPHONE

There are two types of microphones. If you want to record in a noisy environment, pick a unidirectional microphone — it only picks up sounds that are directly in front of it. If you need to move around while recording or want to record all the sounds in a room, pick an omnidirectional microphone.

Most microphones are designed for musicians rather than multimedia explorers. The two types of equipment have different standards. Make sure that the microphone you buy has the correct size jack plug (a ⅛-inch plug is used by multimedia sound cards, but ¼-inch is the standard for musical equipment).

Omnidirectional Microphone

SPEAKERS

For home use or in a quiet office, you can use any small loudspeakers. The little amplifier on the sound card should provide an adequate sound volume. If you are doing a presentation, or if you work in a noisy environment, you'll need amplified speakers. These are loudspeakers that also contain an amplifier powered from batteries or an AC adapter. They are more expensive but give better quality and more powerful sound.

How to Install a Sound Card Safely

Many users get worried at the thought of opening up a PC and installing an expansion card, such as a sound card. Over the next few pages, we'll show you how to do it safely and simply. There are two stages in the process. First you install the hardware (the sound card itself). Then you install a piece of software called a device driver, which allows the PC to communicate with your sound card.

A Hazard to Floppies!
Inside your loudspeakers are magnets. If you place a floppy disk too close to the speaker while it is working, you might accidentally erase what's on your disk. Keep floppy disks several inches away from speakers.

⅛-inch Jack (for Sound Cards)

¼-inch Jack (Standard for Musical Equipment)

Handle Carefully!
When installing a sound card, hold the card by its edges. Do not touch any of its components or the metal connectors on its bottom edge.

INSTALLING THE CARD
Follow these steps to install a sound card in your PC's system unit. Just a few precautions are needed to prevent damage to yourself or the electronics.

1 Turn off your PC.

2 Unplug the power cord and all other cables from the back of your system unit. (In countries such as the UK, where the power cord contains a ground wire, leave the cord attached but *make sure* the power is switched off at the wall socket.)

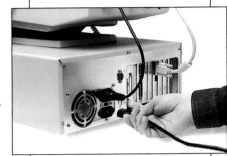

3 Unscrew the chassis screws for the system unit's casing and remove the case (refer to your PC's manual for detailed instructions).

4 Before touching the sound card or anything inside the system unit, ground yourself by touching a metal object outside the computer. (In countries where the power cord contains a ground wire, and if you've kept the power cord attached to the PC, touch a metal plate within the system unit.)

5 Locate a free expansion connector on the motherboard (the large fiberglass circuit board at the bottom of the system unit). At the back of the motherboard is a row of expansion connectors. There will probably be two different lengths of connector. The shorter slots are for 8-bit cards, the longer ones for 16-bit cards. You can install an 8-bit card in a 16-bit slot, but you can't install a 16-bit card in an 8-bit slot.

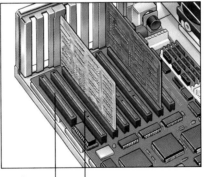

8-bit Connector

16-bit Connector

6 At the back of the free expansion slot, you'll see a small metal plate on the back panel. Undo the screw that holds this plate.

Be Careful in There!
Inside your PC are lots of electronic components that are sensitive to static electricity. Similarly, a sound card could be damaged by a discharge of static electricity. The object of grounding yourself before you pick up your sound card or start delving inside your PC is to discharge any static that may have built up on you.

7 Using both hands, position the sound card vertically so that the metal edge connectors at the bottom of the card are resting on top of the expansion slot (make sure you have a 16-bit slot for a 16-bit card). Then push the card firmly (but not too firmly) downward so that the metal connectors slide into the slot.

8 Screw in the sound card's metal plate.

9 Slide the casing back on, and replace the retaining screws. (If you have also bought an internal CD-ROM drive, you will want to install this first — see page 37.)

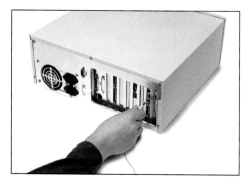

10 Plug your speakers into the connector on the back of the sound card.

11 Reconnect your other cables, plug in the power cord, and turn on your PC.

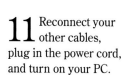

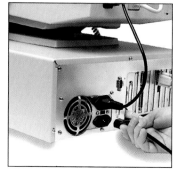

IRQ and DMA Settings

When you install a sound card and an associated driver, you may be prompted to test or set the card's IRQ line, I/O address, or DMA channels — or you may be alerted to a problem with one of these.

■ The *IRQ (interrupt request) line* defines how the sound card alerts the CPU that there is data waiting to be processed. The *DMA channel* is the signal line your sound card uses for data transfer directly to the system's memory. The *I/O address* is used by the CPU to distinguish the sound card from other input/output devices.

■ Often the sound card's default settings for these paths and addresses work fine. But sometimes they clash with existing settings for another expansion card.

■ You can change the IRQ line, DMA channel, and I/O address settings for your sound card by moving little switches on the card — the manual that comes with the card will explain how. If you make changes on the card, you will need to change the device driver settings too. This is done by running a configuration program that comes with the driver software.

■ Don't change any of the settings unless you know what you are doing. Most often, a base I/O address of 220, an IRQ level of 7, and DMA channels of 1 (for 8-bit transfers) and 5 (for 16-bit transfers) will do the trick. If necessary, call your dealer.

Sound Drivers

The sound card can turn numbers into sound or record a sound and turn it into numbers. But it cannot do this by itself — it needs to be told what to do and when to do it. And there is another problem. Controlling how the keyboard, screen, and disk drives work on your PC is the job of the operating system software, which is probably MS-DOS. Unfortunately, most operating systems don't know how to control a sound card. To make the bridge between the operating system and the sound card, you need to install a special piece of software called a *device driver*. The device driver comes on a floppy disk, in the same box as your sound card. You must install it before the sound card will work.

Basically, the device driver lets the operating system know that the sound card is installed and translates the operating system commands into a form the hardware will understand. You may need to install two drivers — one that works with MS-DOS and another that works with Windows.

INSTALLING A DRIVER FOR MS-DOS

Installing a driver for MS-DOS is usually quite straight-forward. A typical procedure is as follows, though you should read any specific instructions that are supplied with the card.

1 Insert the floppy disk containing the driver software into the appropriate floppy disk drive.

`C:\>A:\INSTALL`

2 At the command prompt, type **A:\INSTALL** or **B:\INSTALL** and press Enter. Follow the instructions on the screen. During installation, a special directory is created on your hard disk and some lines are added to your PC's system setup files.

You should now test that the sound card works. Along with the driver software, there is often a configuration and test program, which should be explained in the manual that comes with the sound card. If the card doesn't seem to be working, you may need to configure your card with different IRQ or DMA settings (see opposite). If you find this a little intimidating, or if you get messages that you do not know how to respond to, call your dealer or the card's product support number.

What Does a Device Driver Do?

A device driver is a special program that stays in memory whenever your PC is running. When it detects a command meant for its associated device (such as a sound card), it steps in and controls the hardware. The driver acts as a translator between software and hardware. It is normally supplied by the hardware manufacturer, so it knows how to control your particular hardware device. Operating system software, such as Windows, can ask the driver to carry out an action without having to do the nitty gritty of controlling the hardware itself.

Windows has a special way of talking to drivers called *MCI*, which stands for *media control interface*. This is a set of commands that work with device drivers to control CD-ROM drives and sound cards. The driver translates a standard MCI command into the signals used to control the hardware.

3 Reset your PC by pressing the reset button. The driver is then loaded and takes effect.

RESET

There's No Sound?
Don't forget that once you have installed a new driver, you have to reset your PC to get the driver to work. If you install a new driver for Windows, you'll need to restart Windows.

INSTALLING A DRIVER FOR WINDOWS

Before you can use your sound card with any multimedia software that runs under Windows, you need to tell Windows the type of sound card you have so that it knows how to control it. There may be a special program, included on the floppy disk that came with your sound card, that will automatically set up a Windows driver the next time you open Windows — for example, the Sound Blaster 16 sound card comes with a program called WINSETUP that does just that.

In other cases, you may need to install a driver using the *Drivers* dialog box, which can be reached via Windows Control Panel. Windows 3.1 provides the drivers for several cards.

1 Start Windows, and then double-click on the *Main* group icon in Program Manager.

2 Double-click on the *Control Panel* icon in the *Main* group window.

3 In the *Control Panel* window, double-click on the *Drivers* icon.

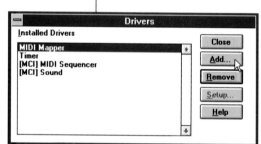

4 In the *Drivers* dialog box, you will see a list of installed drivers. To install a new driver, click on *Add*.

5 In the *Add* dialog box, under *List of Drivers*, Windows displays a list of drivers that are available on the Windows 3.1 program disks. If the driver for your sound card is on the list, click on the name of the driver and then on *OK*. If the driver for your type of sound card does not appear, click on *Unlisted or Updated Driver*, and then on *OK*.

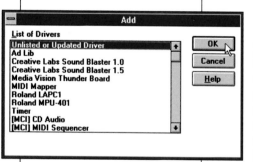

6 In the *Install Driver* dialog box, you will be prompted for either a Windows disk or the disk supplied with the sound card. Insert the correct disk in floppy drive A or B, make sure that A:\ or B:\ appears in the text box, and then click on *OK*.

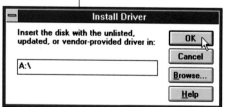

7 Either Windows will load the driver or you will see an *Add Unlisted or Updated Driver* dialog box. In the latter case, select the correct driver and click on *OK*. You'll then need to restart Windows.

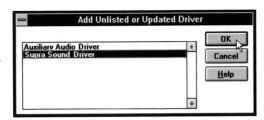

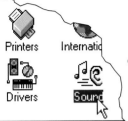

8 To test that the sound driver for Windows is correctly installed, double-click on the *Sound* icon in the *Control Panel* window.

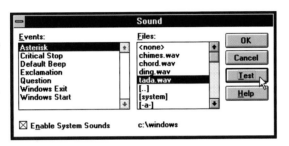

9 In the *Sound* dialog box, select *TADA.WAV* (a small waveform file) under *Files,* and then click on *Test*. You should hear a fanfare from the speakers attached to your sound card.

Stereo Power!
If you have a stereo sound system, you can play your computer's sound through the stereo amplifier. You'll need a special cable and adapter plug to connect the sound card's speaker port or Line Out port to the input labelled AUX on the back of your stereo amplifier.

Making the Connections

You've already connected speakers to the speaker port on the back of your sound card. Now's a good time to look at the other ports and understand their functions. The ports on a typical card are shown below.

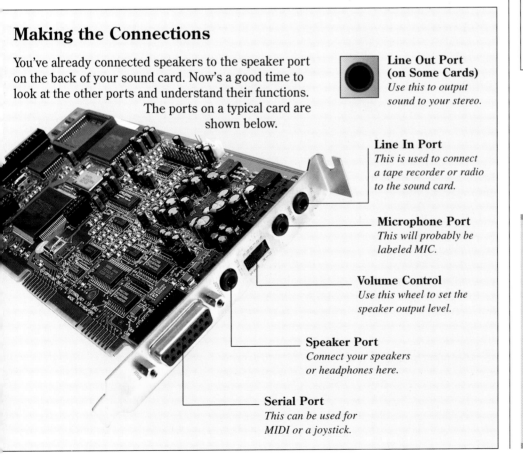

Line Out Port (on Some Cards)
Use this to output sound to your stereo.

Line In Port
This is used to connect a tape recorder or radio to the sound card.

Microphone Port
This will probably be labeled MIC.

Volume Control
Use this wheel to set the speaker output level.

Speaker Port
Connect your speakers or headphones here.

Serial Port
This can be used for MIDI or a joystick.

Plugging Problems?
Some sound cards don't label the connectors on the back. If that's the case with your card, it's a good idea to label them yourself. Take care not to plug your microphone into the speaker port — this could cause damage to the microphone.

CD-ROM Drives

SOUND CARDS ARE AN INDISPENSABLE PART of a multimedia PC, but they give you access only to one part of the multimedia banquet. To take full part in the feast and make use of the abundance of multimedia titles that come on CD-ROM discs, you will need a CD-ROM drive.

CD-ROM Drive

CD-ROM Disc

Committed to Memory

A Mine of Information
The huge storage capacity of a CD-ROM is illustrated by the contents of Microsoft Bookshelf. *This title holds an encyclopedia, a dictionary, a thesaurus, an almanac, an atlas, and two books of quotations on one disc! It is illustrated with over 3,000 sound, image, and animation files.*

CD-ROM stands for Compact Disc Read-Only Memory. As the definition suggests, you can only read data from a CD-ROM disc. Information is stored on the disc during its manufacture; once it has been written to, you can only read the data back from it.

This is the vital difference between CD-ROM discs and hard or floppy disks: you can save your own data onto your PC's hard disk, or onto a floppy disk, but you can only read data back from a CD-ROM disc.

So what purpose does CD-ROM serve? The huge advantage of CD-ROM discs is the amount of data that can be stored on them. A hard disk can normally only manage around 120 MB to 200 MB of data, and the highest capacity floppy disks store a measly 1.44 MB. A CD-ROM disc, however, has a storage capacity of around 650 MB. This is the equivalent of about 170,000 pages of printed text, or about 300 large books! And, as you saw in the last chapter, text storage is just the beginning: it's the space available for graphics, sound, and video that makes CD-ROM discs an essential part of multimedia.

Handle with Care!
Although a CD-ROM disc is protected by a plastic coating, it is still fragile. Always store it in its case, handle it only on the edges, and try to avoid scratching the surface.

What's in Store?

When you compare the amount of information that can be stored on a CD-ROM disc with the amount of data that fits on a 200-MB hard disk, it's easy to see why CD-ROM has taken off.

 Video
A CD-ROM disc can store about 30 minutes of average-quality video clips; a 200-MB hard disk can store only about 10 minutes.

 Audio
You can fit around an hour of high-quality stereo sound on a CD-ROM disc, compared with about 20 minutes on a 200-MB hard disk.

 Graphics
Over 1,000 large (600-KB) bitmapped images will fit on a CD-ROM disc; a 200-MB hard disk will store only about 300 such images.

 Text
A CD-ROM disc can store about 170,000 pages of text; a 200-MB hard disk can hold approximately 50,000 pages.

HOW CD-ROM WORKS

CD-ROM discs not only look exactly the same as the audio compact discs you play in your stereo system, they also use the same technology to store information. In fact, many CD-ROM drives can play music compact discs, although it doesn't work the other way around.

If you hold a CD-ROM disc under a light, you will see a shiny pattern of concentric tracks. These give you a clue as to how CD-ROM works. A spiral track is created on the metal disc, and data is arranged along the track in the form of binary numbers — that is, by using strings of 1s and 0s. A 0 (zero) is indicated by a level area of metal (called a *land*), and a 1 is represented by a pit in the surface of the disc.

The metal layer of binary information is sandwiched between two transparent plastic sheets to protect it from dust and fingerprints.

BLACK HOLES AND LASER BEAMS

When you instruct your CD-ROM drive to read a disc, the drive uses a narrow laser beam to "read" the surface of the metal layer while the disc spins. Where a pit exists in the metal, the light from the laser is not reflected back. Light passing over a level area, however, is reflected back to a light-sensitive component. This information is then routed to the PC.

Writable Drives

Although you've just learned that you can only read from a CD-ROM disc, this is not the whole truth! Writable CD-ROM drives are available, but they're about ten times the price of a normal CD-ROM drive (the blank discs are also expensive). If you develop your own multimedia titles, however, or need to store a lot of data, you might want to rent or buy a writable CD-ROM drive.

Can I Play an Audio CD on My PC?

With the right software on your PC, you can play audio CDs in your CD-ROM drive. However, a stereo will not recognize the text and graphics data on a CD-ROM disc, so you cannot play a CD-ROM disc in your audio CD player. (See page 63 to find out how to play audio CDs in your CD-ROM drive.)

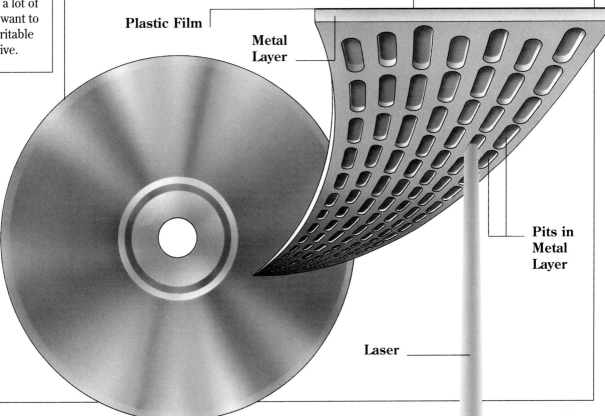

Plastic Film

Metal Layer

Pits in Metal Layer

Laser

Buying Considerations

The first consideration when purchasing a CD-ROM drive is whether to buy an internal or external unit. An internal drive is the same size as a 5¼-inch floppy disk drive and fits into a free 5¼-inch drive bay on the PC. It is powered by the PC through an internal power connector. Internal units are cheaper than external drives because they don't need a separate case, and they also save space on your desk. You will have to buy an external CD-ROM drive if your PC doesn't have any free drive bays.

Two less obvious — but particularly important — factors to consider when buying a CD-ROM drive are *seek time* (sometimes called *access time*) and *data transfer rate*. Both considerations are underpinned by the same fundamental law: the faster the better.

Moveable Multimedia

An external CD-ROM drive is useful if the device will be used on different computers because it is easy to transport between machines.

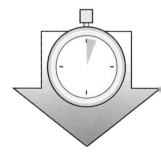

SEEK TIME

The time taken to move the laser beam to the part of the disc you want to read is called the seek time. The very fastest seek times are around a quarter of a second (250 milliseconds, or thousandths of a second) or faster, although a normal time is around one-half to two-thirds of a second (550 to 650 milliseconds).

DATA TRANSFER RATE

Once the laser beam has been positioned over the correct part of the disc, the data has to be read. The amount of data that can be read each second is called the data transfer rate. The first CD-ROM drives transferred data at 150 KB every second, so a large picture file measuring 600 KB in size would take four seconds to be routed from a CD-ROM drive to a PC screen.

The incorporation of data-intensive video clips in multimedia titles increased the attraction of double-speed CD-ROM drives. These can transfer data at 300 KB per second. If you can afford it, you should buy a double-speed CD-ROM drive. Indeed, single-speed drives are on their way to obsolescence.

If you can afford to, you might purchase a triple-speed drive, or one of the very fast *quad-speed drives*, which have a transfer rate of 600 KB per second. Quad-speed drives take only one second to move a 600-KB image from a CD-ROM disc to a PC's hard disk.

Single-Speed Drive

600-KB Image on Disc at 150-KB Transfer Rate

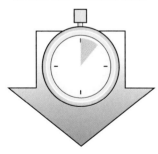

4-Second Transfer Time

Double-Speed Drive

600-KB Image on Disc at 300-KB Transfer Rate

2-Second Transfer Time

Technology Talk

There are a lot of confusing acronyms and many different standards in the CD-ROM world, and the most confusing of these are the guidelines that define how data is stored on a CD-ROM disc.

CD-ROM XA

Until recently, conventional computer data (text and graphics) and sound data had to be recorded on separate sectors of a disc. Getting a PC to display text and graphics on the screen, and at the same time play a sound file, was a slow process because the information had to be accessed from two different sources and then mixed together in the PC's memory.

The new *CD-ROM XA* (extended architecture) standard allows computer data and audio signals to be recorded on the same sector of a CD-ROM disc. If you want to protect your purchase from obsolescence, buy a CD-ROM drive that supports CD-ROM XA. Be careful, though: A few drives labelled "XA-ready" actually need extra hardware components before they can read XA discs.

MULTISESSION CAPABILITIES

Some CD-ROM drives also boast of supporting "multisession discs." *Multisession-compatible drives* were originally developed by Kodak for its PhotoCD system (see page 84 for more on PhotoCD), and such drives can read a disc that has been recorded in several different sessions rather than all at once. To read a PhotoCD disc, you'll need a drive that is multisession compatible and contains the necessary PhotoCD decoder.

CD-ROM Sector

Sound and Image in Separate Sectors

CD-ROM XA Sector

Sound and Image in a Single Sector

What's the Difference?

Although a CD-ROM is superior to a hard disk in terms of storage capacity, there is a comparative speed disadvantage in terms of running software. The read head of a hard disk moves across the surface of the disk much faster than a laser beam moves across the CD-ROM disc, so hard disks are much quicker at information retrieval. The average access time of a hard disk is 20 milliseconds, with an average data transfer rate of around 2 to 3 MB per second — a good deal faster than CD-ROM drive speeds.

When using CD-ROM software, you will have to get used to the slower pace. Game players will find it especially noticeable and might prefer to buy their games on floppy disks to install on their hard disks.

Installing a CD-ROM Drive

Port for Internal CD-ROM Drive

Port for External CD-ROM Drive

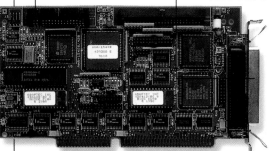

Controlling Interest
Interface cards (also called controllers) provide a port for connecting a CD-ROM drive to a PC. The connection cable you use depends on whether you buy an internal or external drive.

There are several steps to installing a CD-ROM drive. Whether you have bought an internal or an external drive, you first need to establish an interface between the CD-ROM drive and your PC. Unless your sound card has a built-in CD-ROM interface (see below), this will mean inserting a special controller card, called an *interface card*, into a free expansion slot inside your PC. You then plug the CD-ROM drive into the interface card. Finally, you install a device driver in your machine.

An interface card provides the physical and electrical connection between a hardware device — in this case, your CD-ROM drive — and a PC. The most common type of interface is called *SCSI*. This is pronounced "scuzzy" and stands for Small Computer Systems Interface.

When choosing a SCSI card, try to buy a 16-bit *SCSI-2* card. SCSI-2 is the newer standard and it is faster than plain SCSI. A 16-bit card will also speed up the transfer of data from the CD-ROM drive.

CD-ROM AND SOUND CARD CONNECTIONS

Some sound cards have a built-in CD-ROM interface, and this allows you to plug a CD-ROM drive into the sound card rather than buying a separate SCSI connector. If you have a sound card in your PC, check the manual to see if it offers a CD-ROM interface. Some sound cards have a proprietary interface that accepts only certain makes of CD-ROM drives; others offer a SCSI interface that does not limit you in your choice of CD-ROM drives.

If you buy an upgrade kit, the sound card will include an integral interface for the CD-ROM drive.

INSTALLATION STEPS

If you have bought an upgrade kit, or if your PC has a sound card that contains a built-in CD-ROM interface, follow the steps on page 43 in the section on upgrading. If you need to insert an interface card yourself, follow steps 1 through 8 on pages 27 and 28 for installing a sound card (but substitute the words "interface card" for "sound card").

Once the interface card has been fitted in an expansion slot, follow the steps on the opposite page to install an internal CD-ROM drive on your PC. If you have an external drive, follow the steps under "How to Install an External CD-ROM Drive" on page 38.

Check Whether the Card Is Included
When you buy a CD-ROM drive, always check whether it comes with an interface card. Some manufacturers of CD-ROM drives make their own proprietary interface cards. If you buy a drive with a proprietary interface, the card will come with the drive. If the drive you buy uses a SCSI connector, however, you might need to buy the SCSI interface card separately.

Audio Cable

Data Cable

Power Connector

The Internal Drive Back Panel

Power Connector
One of the power cables that protrudes from the PC's power supply is plugged into this connector.

Audio Connector
Some CD-ROM drives offer a facility for connecting the drive's audio output directly to a sound card.

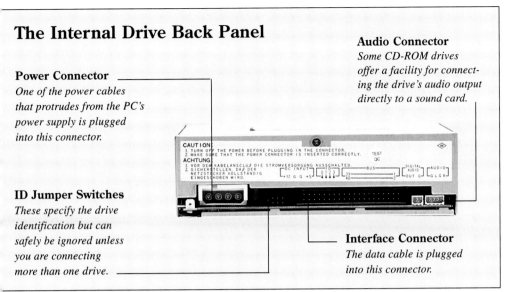

ID Jumper Switches
These specify the drive identification but can safely be ignored unless you are connecting more than one drive.

Interface Connector
The data cable is plugged into this connector.

I Don't Have a Spare Power Cable!
PCs have from two to four power cables connected to the internal power supply box. Each floppy drive needs to use one of these cables, so if you have two power cables and two floppy drives, you will not have a spare one for your CD-ROM drive. In this case, buy a "Y" adapter so you can power the CD-ROM drive and both of your floppy drives.

How to Install an Internal CD-ROM Drive

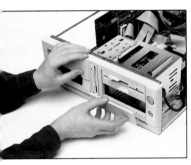

1 Unplug the PC as described on page 27. Remove the plate in front of the free 5¼-inch drive bay.

2 Slide the internal CD-ROM drive into the drive bay.

3 Connect the data cable (the wide cable) to the interface card; use the data cable connector on the face of the card, not the one on the back of the card.

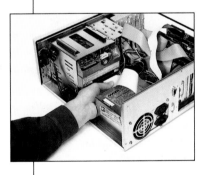

4 Now attach the other end of the data cable to the interface connector at the back of the CD-ROM drive.

5 Connect a spare power cable protruding from the PC's power supply box to the CD-ROM drive. Now screw the CD-ROM drive securely into place in the drive bay.

6 Replace the system unit's case and plug the machine into the wall outlet.

The External Drive Back Panel

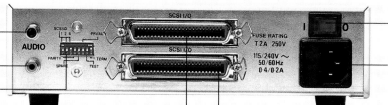

Audio Line Connectors
For connecting the drive to a stereo system.

ID Jumper Switches
These specify the drive identification but can safely be ignored unless you have more than one drive.

Power Switch

Power Connector
This connects the drive to a wall socket.

Interface Connectors
The data cable is plugged into one of these connectors — it doesn't matter which one you choose. The spare connector (if present) is used only if you want to daisy-chain other devices to the interface connector.

How to Install an External CD-ROM Drive

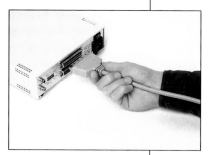

1 Connect the data cable to the interface connector at the back of the CD-ROM drive.

2 Attach the other end of the data cable to the connector at the back of the interface card.

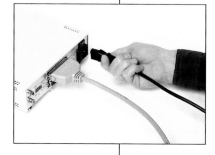

3 Plug the power cord into the CD-ROM drive, and then plug the drive into the wall socket.

Installing the Software

As with the sound card, you need to tell MS-DOS that it has a new piece of hardware to control, so drivers for the CD-ROM drive must be installed (see page 29 for an explanation of drivers).

Typically, you insert the floppy disk supplied with the CD-ROM drive into floppy disk drive A or B, and then type **A:\INSTALL** or **B:\INSTALL** at the command prompt. Press Enter, and then follow the instructions that appear on your screen. Don't forget that you have to reset the machine for the driver to take effect.

Duelling Drivers!
Unfortunately, installing an interface controller in a PC that already has a sound card sometimes leads to a clash of IRQ or DMA settings. (See page 28 for an explanation of IRQ and DMA settings.) You can easily change the settings for the CD-ROM drive by following the instructions in the manual. If you don't feel confident about doing it yourself, call your dealer for expert help.

THE NAME OF THE DRIVE

When you add a CD-ROM drive to your PC, it normally becomes the next letter in the alphabet after the hard disk drive. If your hard disk is C, the CD-ROM drive will be D, although if you are connected to a network the drive letter might be different.

Once you have installed your CD-ROM drive, start Windows and go into the File Manager. You will see the letter that represents your CD-ROM drive next to the icon that is used to represent it — a picture of a drive with a disc sticking out of it.

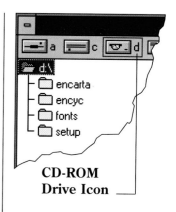

CD-ROM Drive Icon

Using a CD-ROM Drive

Except for the fact that you cannot save data to it, a CD-ROM drive is controlled in much the same way as a floppy disk drive. You place the disc in its drive and then access the information stored on it by switching to the CD-ROM drive.

LOADING DISCS

There are two ways to insert a disc into the CD-ROM drive, depending on the type of drive you have. The choice is between a caddy system and a tray system.

The tray system is the most convenient option. It works just like a stereo music CD player in that you place the CD-ROM disc onto a small tray and push it gently into the drive. Some drives have a motorized loading system that requires only a slight push on the tray for smooth loading.

With the caddy system, you have to insert the disc into a plastic cartridge (a caddy) and then push the caddy into the drive. Caddy-based systems are usually more expensive than tray-based drives, but they do provide more protection against dust, which is useful if you are in a particularly dusty or smoky environment.

Printed Side Up
Like audio CDs, one side of a CD-ROM disc is printed with the title of the disc, and the other side is clear. To load the disc, hold it by its edges (try to avoid touching the surface) and place it printed side up onto the drive tray.

How to Load a CD-ROM Caddy

1 Place the disc inside the plastic caddy.

2 Insert the caddy into the CD-ROM drive.

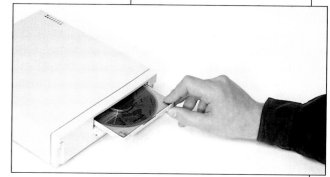

Using a CD-ROM Disc

Dust is a major problem with discs. A particle of dust on a disc's surface can cause an error when the drive tries to read the data on the disc. Always keep discs in their protective cases when you are not using them.

If you want to clean a disc, breathe on the surface, and then use a soft, lint-free cloth (not tissue) to gently wipe the surface clean.

DON'T TOUCH!

Your fingers carry grease and dirt, which could scratch or dirty the surface of a CD-ROM disc. Always hold the disc by its edges and avoid touching the flat surface. Some people prefer to handle a disc by using an index finger on the inside rim and a thumb on the outer edge.

INSTALLING A DISC

The first time you use a multimedia title or software package available on CD-ROM, you will usually have to run an install program. This normally copies some essential program files from the CD-ROM onto your hard disk, so the more titles you install, the more your hard disk will fill up. Most of a title's files, including all the large graphics and sound files, stay on the CD-ROM disc, however, so the disc has to be in the CD-ROM drive when the program is run. You may find that a few titles don't install any files onto your hard disk.

SLOW MOTION, FAST MOTION

Some titles allow you to choose how many files to load onto your hard disk. During the installation of these titles, a window will appear detailing how much disk space the recommended option will take up. You will then be given the option of choosing a less disk-hungry path.

Because CD-ROM drives are much slower than hard disk drives, animation and video files tend to look a little slow and jerky when played directly from a CD-ROM drive. Loading animation files onto your hard disk makes them run faster. The big drawback with loading files onto your hard disk is the amount of space they take up. Video and animation files, especially, are very greedy, although the space they take up is compensated for by much smoother movement.

Battles for Space
Installing the animation from Battle Chess *(above) onto your hard disk takes up 32 MB of disk space, but the battle scenes (below) run more smoothly.*

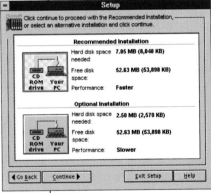

Room for Information
Microsoft Encarta *tells you how much free space you have on your hard disk, and then gives you two installation options. The recommended option installs 7.85 MB on your hard disk; the alternative will only take up 2.5 MB of space.*

Directories in MS-DOS
When you have switched to the CD-ROM drive, you can use the DIR command to see what's stored on a disc.

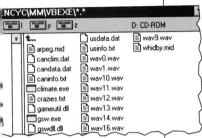

File Extensions
You can recognize sound files by their WAV and MID extensions.

**Icons for
Copying and
Printing Files**

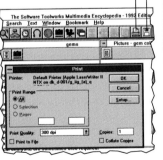

Carbon Copies
The Software Toolworks Multimedia Encyclopedia *lets you send articles and pictures directly to a printer or copy them to the Windows Clipboard.*

CONTROLLING THE DISC WITH MS-DOS

Most normal MS-DOS commands work with a CD-ROM drive. To see what is on a disc, insert the disc into the CD-ROM drive and switch to the drive by typing the drive letter (usually D) and a colon and pressing Enter. Then use the MS-DOS command DIR to see a list of files and directories.

To install a title that runs under MS-DOS, put the disc in the CD-ROM drive, switch to that drive, and then type **INSTALL** and press Enter. From there, simply follow the on-screen instructions; once installation is complete, you will be told what to type at the command prompt to launch the title. Some titles don't install any data on your hard disk. The accompanying manual will tell you how to start the title.

CONTROLLING THE DISC IN WINDOWS

Like hard and floppy disks, CD-ROM discs that run under Windows are controlled by the File Manager. To see what is stored on a disc, open File Manager and click on the icon that indicates your CD-ROM drive. The directory tree displays all the subdirectories and files on the disc.

Depending on what is on the disc you use, you will probably see some new file extensions. If sound files are present, you will see WAV or MID extensions; video clips are often indicated by an AVI extension.

To install a title that runs under Windows, double-click on the SETUP.EXE file in the *File Manager* window, and then follow the instructions that appear on your screen.

Copying CD-ROM Files

Many multimedia titles allow you to copy files to your hard disk or to a specified printer. Before doing so, check any copyright information that comes with the disk (see page 121 for more information on copyright).

If you know the name of the file you want to copy to your hard disk, you can use Windows' drag and drop facility by displaying the files in the File Manager and then dragging the file you want to copy over the icon for drive C. When you let go of the mouse button, Windows will copy the file to drive C.

Alternatively, from the MS-DOS command prompt, you can use the DIR command to obtain a list of files and directories on a CD-ROM, and then use the COPY command to copy files to your hard disk.

What's in a Name?
Once Space Adventure *has been installed on the hard disk, you are informed what to type at the command prompt to play the title.*

Easy Installation
Double-click on the SETUP.EXE file to install a Windows title.

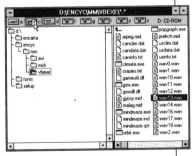

Drag and Drop
Copying files is easy with the Windows drag and drop facility.

Upgrade Kits

IF YOU WANT TO UPGRADE YOUR EXISTING PC TO A MULTIMEDIA PC, one of the most convenient ways to do it is to buy an upgrade kit. An upgrade kit comprises a sound card with a built-in CD-ROM interface, a CD-ROM drive, and — sometimes — a number of optional extras like speakers, a microphone, and perhaps some multimedia titles. What an upgrade kit doesn't include is any equipment to improve your PC's performance — for that, you might need to buy some extra components (see page 44 for more information on performance upgrades).

(see page 44 for more information on performance upgrades)

What Is the MPC Specification?
When you shop for an upgrade kit, you will find that many of them display an *MPC* logo. This logo certifies that the kit meets or exceeds the specifications of the Multimedia PC Council. The MPC logo indicates that the equipment conforms to certain minimum specifications and that it can be used to run multimedia software. However, it is no guarantee of performance: There can be big differences between two MPC-approved devices, so study the specifications carefully.

Speakers — **Sound Card**

CD-ROM Drive

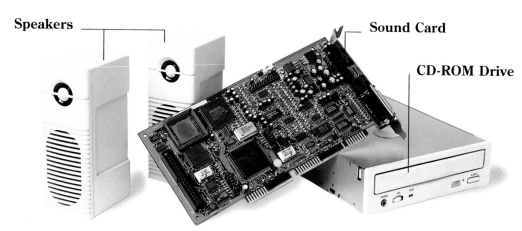

Two Ways to Upgrade

Buying an upgrade kit is usually cheaper than buying the components separately, mainly because the CD-ROM interface is built into the sound card. This also makes upgrade kits easier to install; the CD-ROM drive doesn't have an interface card of its own, so you won't have any problems with clashing interrupt request settings between the two cards.

However, installing the sound/CD-ROM drive controller combination card means that you can't replace one half of the kit — for instance, the sound card — without changing the other half as well.

INTEGRATED UPGRADE KITS
A few companies offer integrated upgrade kits, with many of the multimedia components, like the CD-ROM drive and speakers, built into a single unit. An example is the Memphis multimedia upgrade system from Media Vision. Such a kit usually plugs into a wall socket separately, and the modular design requires fewer connection cables. Some of these units can be connected to stereos and operate as stand-alone audio CD players.

Memphis Multimedia Upgrade System

CD-ROM Drive

Speaker

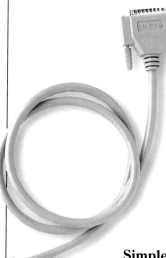

Simple Connections
Integrated upgrade kits are usually connected to the PC via a single cable, making the installation process a little easier.

Installing an Upgrade Kit

The first part of installing an upgrade kit involves inserting the sound/CD-ROM drive controller card into a free expansion slot on the motherboard. To do this, follow steps 1 through 8 for installing a sound card on pages 27 to 28. Once the card is in an expansion slot, follow the steps below.

Audio Cable

CD-ROM Drive Interface

Sound/CD-ROM Drive Controller Card

Data Cable

Installing a CD-ROM Drive and Connecting it to a Controller Card

Power Connector

Data Cable

1 Remove the plate in front of the empty 5¼-inch drive bay, slide the internal CD-ROM drive into the bay, and screw it securely into place. Now follow the kit's instructions. Typically, you first connect the data cable (that's the wide cable) to the CD-ROM interface on the controller card. Then you attach the other end of the data cable to the interface connector at the back of the CD-ROM drive.

2 Connect one of the spare power cables protruding from the PC's power supply box to the CD-ROM drive.

Audio Cable

3 If an audio cable is supplied, connect this to the controller card and then to the CD-ROM drive. Replace the PC's case and plug the machine into the electrical outlet. Before switching the power on, plug the speakers into the jack on the back panel of the controller card.

Power Cable

Installing the MS-DOS Drivers

Installing the Windows Driver

Installing the Software

Most upgrade kits come with one or more software installation disks for the sound card and the CD-ROM drive. Install the software by putting the first disk into a floppy disk drive and typing **A:\INSTALL** or **B:\INSTALL** at the MS-DOS prompt. When you press Enter, you will be given a series of instructions to follow.

Windows also needs to be informed of the sound card's presence. Sometimes this is done automatically the next time you start Windows. Consult your manual; if you need to install the Windows driver yourself, follow the instructions for installing the driver on page 30.

Once installation of the sound card and CD-ROM software is complete, reset the PC to allow the changes to take effect.

Performance Upgrades

YOU ARE NOW FAMILIAR WITH the new components you should install to start exploring multimedia. However, if your PC itself is not up to par, it may have trouble running multimedia titles. This is because a multimedia machine needs to satisfy certain performance requirements; if it doesn't, you might find that your choice of multimedia software is limited or that the software you buy runs slowly.

In addition to a sound card and a CD-ROM player, running multimedia software also requires a PC with the following minimum specifications: 4 MB of memory, a hard disk with a storage capacity of at least 80 MB, and an 80386 microprocessor. In each instance, the higher you go above the minimum specification, the better.

Anyone can upgrade a PC's memory, hard disk, or processor given the appropriate instructions, but there is insufficient space to include the full details here. If you want to upgrade but are unsure how to do so, ask an expert for help.

Hard Disk

Microprocessor

Memory Chips (RAM)

A Memory for Multimedia

When you turn on your PC and work with data, the machine stores the information you use in random access memory (*RAM*). Generally, the more RAM you have, the faster your machine will work.

You can increase your PC's RAM by purchasing a *SIMM* (single in-line memory module), which is a package of chips mounted together on one plug-in card. A SIMM can carry from 1 MB to 16 MB of RAM. Most PCs offer eight SIMM slots on the motherboard. Usually, some of these are filled by the manufacturer and the others are left free for you to upgrade memory.

SIMM Card

RAM Chip

ADDING RAM
To add memory, you need to take into account the size and speed of the RAM already installed in your PC and the size of the connector used by the SIMM slots. If you add incompatible SIMMs, you could find that your PC doesn't work properly or may not work at all. Once you have added RAM, you must inform your PC that it has more memory to work with. You do this by running the PC's setup program and changing the relevant settings.

Occupied SIMM Slots on the Motherboard

Free SIMM Slots on the Motherboard

What About the Microprocessor?
The microprocessor controls all the information processing in a computer, so the more powerful it is, the faster your software will run. Some PCs allow you to upgrade the microprocessor — for instance, to turn an 80386 into an 80486 — by replacing the chip.

I Don't Have a Spare Drive Bay!
If your machine doesn't have space for another internal disk drive, you can always buy an external drive. This plugs into the wall socket separately. External hard drives are usually added to a PC through a SCSI interface (see page 36 for more on the SCSI interface). Some external drives can be connected to the computer's parallel port, but these are slower.

Daisy-Chaining Two Internal Hard Disk Drives

Hard Disks

Data Cable

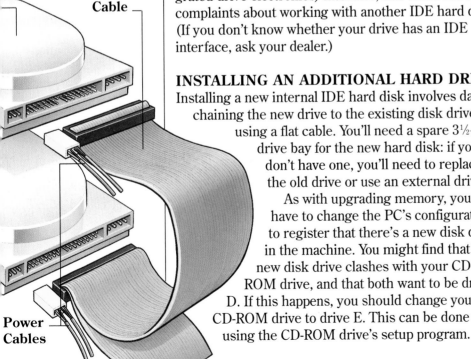

Power Cables

A Tight Fit

When you have finished working on a PC and you switch it off, the information in RAM is lost forever — unless you save it to a disk (usually your hard disk). As you have seen, most multimedia titles also save some information on your hard disk during installation, so the more space you have for storing files, the better.

This is especially true if you intend to experiment with making your own multimedia. You will find the free space on your hard disk diminishing as fast as your library of sound and picture files grows. If you don't want to resort to storing files on floppy disks, you will need to consider upgrading your hard disk.

THE HARD FACTS ABOUT DISK DRIVES

Before upgrading your hard disk, think carefully about the amount of storage space you require. As disk capacity goes up, the cost per megabyte goes down, so it pays to buy a large drive. Besides, you can be sure that you will need more storage space than you think!

You will also need to consider whether you want to replace your present drive completely or supplement it with an additional drive. You might not have the choice: if your PC is several years old, it might prove impossible to find a hard disk that will work alongside the original one. In this case, it would be best to retire the old drive and replace it with a new model.

Newer hard disk drives usually have an *IDE* (integrated drive electronics) interface, and these have no complaints about working with another IDE hard drive. (If you don't know whether your drive has an IDE interface, ask your dealer.)

INSTALLING AN ADDITIONAL HARD DRIVE

Installing a new internal IDE hard disk involves daisy-chaining the new drive to the existing disk drive using a flat cable. You'll need a spare 3½-inch drive bay for the new hard disk: if you don't have one, you'll need to replace the old drive or use an external drive.

As with upgrading memory, you will have to change the PC's configuration to register that there's a new disk drive in the machine. You might find that the new disk drive clashes with your CD-ROM drive, and that both want to be drive D. If this happens, you should change your CD-ROM drive to drive E. This can be done using the CD-ROM drive's setup program.

The Soft Option
If you need more disk storage space, there is an alternative to upgrading your hard disk. Disk compression programs are available that will compress the data stored on a hard disk — in some cases almost doubling the capacity of the drive. You might want to make use of one of these utilities before you rush out and buy an extra hard disk.

Monitors and Display

Y OU CAN ENJOY THE POWER AND BEAUTY of multimedia to its fullest only if your PC can display sharp and colorful images. The quality of the images you'll see depends both on the monitor and on the display adapter card inside your PC. In this section, you'll find out how monitors and display adapters work and what the different specifications mean.

How Monitors Work

Monitors display color images by using combinations of three primary colors. At the back of the monitor are three electron guns — one each for red, green, and blue — that produce fine electron beams as they respond to signals from the *display adapter card* inside the PC. The image on the screen is made up of thousands of elements called *pixels*. A pixel consists of a group of phosphor dots that glow red, green, or blue as they are struck by the electron beams. The *resolution*, or sharpness, of the screen display depends on the number of pixels used for that display — the more pixels, the higher the resolution.

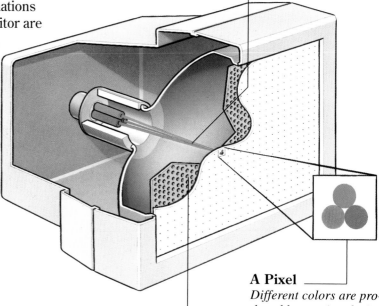

Electron Beams
The three beams scan horizontally across the monitor screen, moving down one line at a time. The entire screen is scanned at least 60 times every second.

A Pixel
Different colors are produced by varying the intensities of the electron beams that hit the dots in a pixel. For example, if the red and blue dots are struck by high-intensity beams, and the green dot is off, the pixel appears purple.

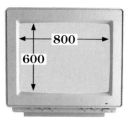

VGA Monitor
Until recently, the industry standard for monitors was VGA (Video Graphics Array). A VGA monitor has a maximum resolution of 640-by-480 — it can display a maximum of 640 pixels horizontally on each line and 480 lines vertically.

SVGA Monitor
Today, the VGA standard has been superseded by SVGA (super VGA). Most SVGA monitors display either 800 pixels horizontally and 600 lines vertically or 1,024 pixels horizontally and 768 lines vertically.

Shadow Mask
This thin metal sheet contains tiny holes that correspond to the positions of dots on the screen. The mask prevents stray electrons from striking adjacent dots and blurring the image.

THE DISPLAY ADAPTER CARD

The display adapter card (also called the video card or graphics card) stores and continuously updates the images displayed on your monitor. The card receives signals from other parts of the computer, assimilates the signals if necessary, and builds an image that it passes to the monitor for display. To utilize the maximum resolution of a monitor, you need a display adapter card that can support that resolution. Thus you'll need an SVGA adapter card if you want to use the maximum resolution of an SVGA monitor.

PIXELS AND COLORS

Information about the grid of pixels on the monitor screen is stored on special memory chips (called *video RAM*) on the display adapter card. The information about each pixel is a record of the pixel's color, encoded as a number. If the data for each pixel is stored in eight bits (one byte) of memory, any one of 256 colors can be assigned to each pixel. This is called an 8-bit color display or a *color depth* of 256 colors.

Although an 8-bit color display is fine for most purposes, if you want to see the subtle tones in photographs you really need a display adapter that can handle two or three bytes for each pixel. Each pixel in a 16-bit (two bytes per pixel) color display can be any one of 65,536 different colors. In a 24-bit (three bytes per pixel) display, each pixel can be any one of 16.77 million different colors! At the other end of the scale is 4-bit color, which displays only 16 colors.

Take Your Pic
The images below show a photograph as it would appear on a monitor screen using three different color depths but the same resolution in each case.

**16 Colors
(4-bit color)**

**256 Colors
(8-bit color)**

**65,536 Colors
(16-bit color)**

THE MEMORY PROBLEM

Being able to display thousands or millions of colors on screen sounds great, but there's a problem: the amount of video RAM available. An image with a resolution of 800-by-600 has 480,000 pixels. If you want 256 colors, allocating one byte of memory per pixel, you'd need a display adapter with 480 KB of video RAM for the image. If you want 16.77 million different colors — that's three bytes per pixel — you'd need 1.44 MB of video RAM just to display one image!

As a general rule, unless you invest in a display adapter with large amounts of video RAM (2 MB or more), you'll find there's a trade-off between resolution and the number of colors available — you can either have a high-resolution image with just a few colors or a low-resolution image with thousands of colors.

Choosing Your Resolution

Some monitor/adapter card combinations give you a choice of resolutions and color depths. For example, with an SVGA monitor and adapter card that can display 1024-by-768 pixels, you can also use resolutions of 800-by-600 or 640-by-480 if you wish. You might also be able to switch between 16 and 256 or more colors. To change the display mode, you need to change the *video driver* — special software that acts as an interface between your PC's operating system and your display adapter (see page 49).

What's the Dot Pitch?

The *dot pitch* is the distance between the groups of red, green, and blue dots on the inside of the monitor. The smaller the dot pitch, the sharper the images. Most monitors have a dot pitch of around .28 mm. The better quality monitors have a dot pitch of .24 mm.

Monitor Size

The two most popular sizes for monitors are 14-inch and 15-inch. A 14-inch monitor is fine for VGA displays (640-by-480) but is a little squashed for SVGA (800-by-600). A 15-inch monitor is just right for 800-by-600, but if you want to use higher resolution images (1024-by-768), you really need a 17-inch monitor. (The image you see on the screen above is from Compton's Interactive Encyclopedia.*)*

Choosing Your System

You've seen how monitors work and how high resolution images with a lot of colors need a lot of memory. Now you can start choosing the best graphics system for your multimedia PC.

VGA OR SVGA?

With a VGA setup you have a maximum resolution of 640-by-480 pixels and a maximum of 256 colors. For your multimedia experiments, it's likely that you're eventually going to want a higher resolution and more colors, especially if you intend to display photographic images on screen, so you'll do best with an SVGA monitor and adapter card.

MEMORY AND SPEED

Next, be sure that your display adapter has enough memory or that extra memory can be added. With 1 MB of video RAM, you can display 256 colors at the highest resolutions (1024-by-768) or up to 24-bit graphics (16.77 million colors) at a resolution of 640-by-480. With 2 MB of video RAM, you can display 24-bit graphics at a resolution of 800-by-600.

The display adapter can be a bottleneck for data. You need a display adapter with at least a 16-bit interface, which needs a 16-bit expansion slot. For the fastest transfers, consider a local bus interface — a new standard that connects the display adapter directly to the central processing unit. Many PCs come with a Windows accelerator card — sometimes this is just a display adapter with more video RAM, sometimes it's a card with a local bus interface. It should speed up the display of graphics.

Refresh Frequency

The refresh frequency is the number of times per second that the electron beams scan the whole screen. The minimum you should consider is 72 Hz — the image is redrawn 72 times each second. Any less and you could see flickering and get a headache. Be sure your monitor has a refresh rate of 72 Hz with the resolutions and color depths you intend to use.

Interlaced and Noninterlaced Monitors

These two types of monitors differ in the way they draw the image on the screen. *Interlaced* monitors tend to have an annoying flicker, so a *noninterlaced* monitor is preferable. Some monitors offer a non-interlaced display up to a resolution of 800-by-600, but an interlaced display at a resolution of 1024-by-768. If you can, get a monitor that uses a noninterlaced 72 Hz vertical refresh rate at all resolutions.

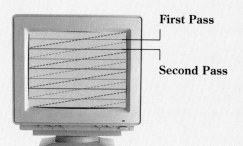

First Pass

Second Pass

Interlaced Monitor

An interlaced monitor draws every other line of an image and then fills in the odd lines on the second pass. In effect, it takes two passes to draw the entire image.

Noninterlaced Monitor

A noninterlaced monitor draws each consecutive line and so gives a more stable image. These monitors cost more, but the additional expense is worth it.

Smaller Window?
Note that a high-specification graphics system won't help with all of your software. For example, when some multimedia titles are run at high resolutions, you may find that the program window shrinks to fill a smaller part of the screen.

Nevertheless, the higher the capacity of your graphics system, the more likely it is that you will be able to take advantage of multimedia titles.

Setting Up

If you want to use multimedia software based on Windows, you may have to configure Windows to use the display adapter at the resolution you desire. This may mean changing the video driver or installing a new driver. Windows 3.1 provides generic drivers for a few display modes, including both VGA (640-by-480) and SVGA (800-by-600) at a color depth of 16 colors. Windows 3.11 provides extra drivers for 256 colors at various resolutions. For higher resolutions or more colors, you may need to install a driver from a disk supplied with the display adapter. Check first to determine the display modes your monitor supports.

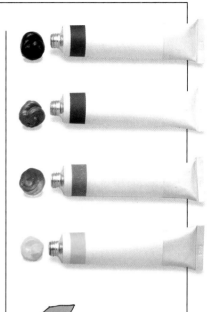

Changing the Display for Windows-Based Software

1 Double-click on the *Windows Setup* icon in the *Main* group window.

2 In the *Windows Setup* dialog box, the current display mode is shown.

3 If you want to change the display, choose *Change System Settings* from the *Options* menu. Click on the down arrow next to the *Display* list box. You can then scroll through a list of possible display modes.

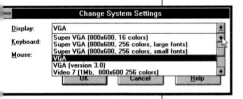

4 Choose a display mode supported by one of the drivers supplied with Windows, or click on *Other display (Requires disk from OEM)*. Follow the instructions on the screen.

5 Once the driver for the new display mode is set up, you'll need to restart Windows for the change to take effect.

No Display!
If you try to change to a display mode that your monitor does not support, you may find that you cannot restart Windows or that the display flickers wildly. If that happens, reset your PC, change to the WINDOWS directory at the MS-DOS command prompt, type **SETUP**, press Enter, and, under *System Information*, change your display back to what it was previously.

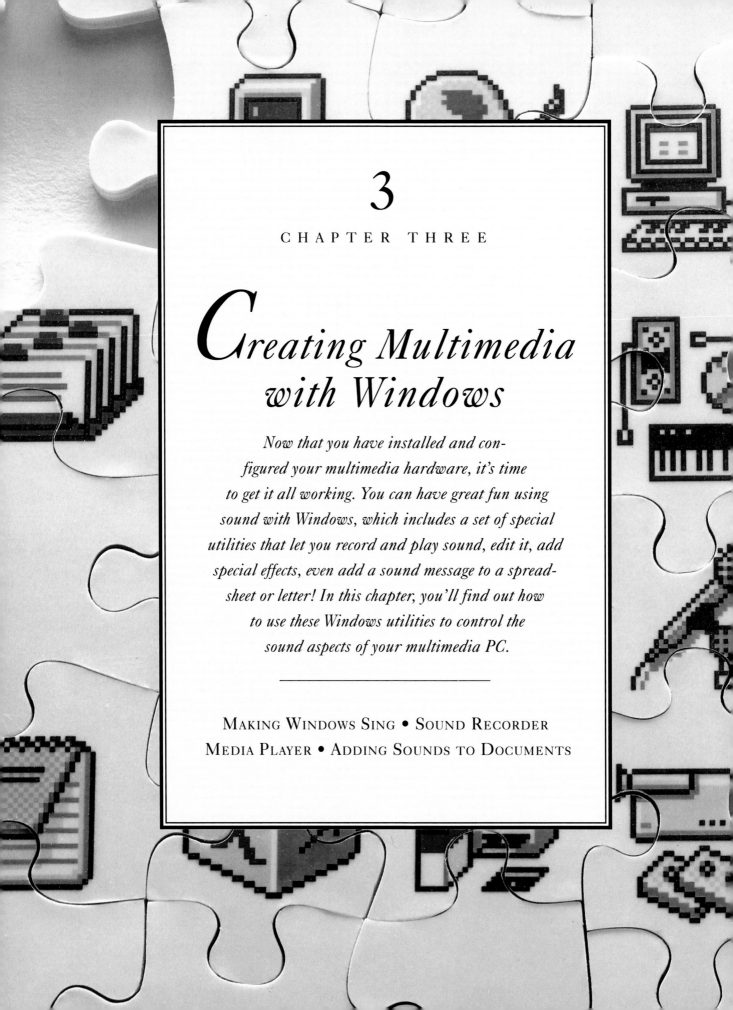

3

CHAPTER THREE

Creating Multimedia with Windows

Now that you have installed and configured your multimedia hardware, it's time to get it all working. You can have great fun using sound with Windows, which includes a set of special utilities that let you record and play sound, edit it, add special effects, even add a sound message to a spreadsheet or letter! In this chapter, you'll find out how to use these Windows utilities to control the sound aspects of your multimedia PC.

MAKING WINDOWS SING • SOUND RECORDER
MEDIA PLAYER • ADDING SOUNDS TO DOCUMENTS

MAKING WINDOWS SING *52*

Learn how to assign sounds to some common Windows events — for example, you can have a trumpet fanfare or a "ding" play when you open Windows, and a warning chime when you make a mistake.

SOUND RECORDER *54*

With the Sound Recorder utility active and a microphone plugged into your sound card, you'll soon be making professional-sounding recordings! Find out how to record sound files, how to edit and combine them, and how to add special effects.

MEDIA PLAYER *62*

When you work with Media Player, it's as if you have the controls to a tape deck, CD-player, or VCR right there on your computer screen. Learn how to use Media Player to play sound and video files or to control an audio CD-ROM drive.

ADDING SOUNDS TO DOCUMENTS *64*

Find out how to use Windows object linking and embedding (OLE) features to add voice annotations or musical messages to any document. This is the beginning of real multimedia creation!

Making Windows Sing

W INDOWS HAS MANY FEATURES that can help you get the most from your multimedia hardware. Once you've installed a sound card (using the technique we showed you in the last chapter), you can start using these features. As a first step, you can assign some sounds such as chimes and fanfares to a variety of Windows events.

The Media Control Interface

Windows has a special set of commands that it uses to control multimedia devices such as sound cards. This command set is called the media control interface (MCI). MCI might sound technical, but it lets you do some neat tricks with Windows.

Every time an important Windows event happens, Windows sends out an MCI command that tells the hardware what it's doing. You can use these messages to generate sounds — all you need to do is assign some sounds, stored as waveform files on your hard disk, to particular Windows events. To start with, you can assign some sounds provided by Windows itself.

CHIMES.WAV

Sounds like a doorbell chime

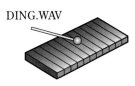

DING.WAV

Sounds like a single note on a xylophone

CHORD.WAV

Sounds like a single chord on a piano

TADA.WAV

Sounds like a horn fanfare

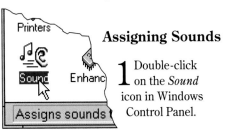

Assigning Sounds

1 Double-click on the *Sound* icon in Windows Control Panel.

Events That Can Cause a Sound to Play

2 The *Sound* dialog box is displayed. If the sound files listed on the right are grayed out, you cannot play or assign any sounds because your sound card is not properly installed for Windows. Look back at page 30 to determine whether you have installed the driver for Windows.

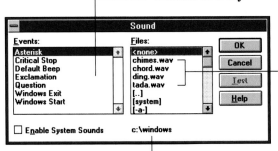

Sound Files in the Current Directory
Only sound files with a WAV extension are displayed.

Current Directory

3 Test the sound files provided with Windows. Click once to select one of the sound files on the right, and then click on the *Test* button. You should hear the sound. Now try out the rest of the sounds.

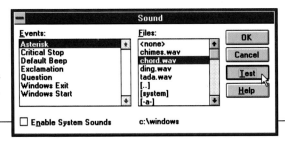

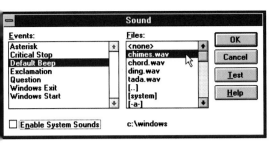

4 Choose *Default Beep* from the list on the left-hand side. This event warns you that you have performed an action that Windows doesn't recognize. Select one of the sound files in the right-hand list — for example, CHIMES.WAV.

5 Click on the *Enable System Sounds* option box in the lower left-hand side of the window. When this option is enabled (the box has an "x" in it), the sounds you assign to each event will be played. If this option is disabled, none of the sounds assigned to events (except *Windows Start* and *Windows Exit*) will be played. To confirm that you want the default beep to be a chime, click on *OK*. Then close the *Control Panel* window.

Now test the default beep. One way to do this is to open any Windows application, like Paintbrush, choose *Open* from the *File* menu, and then click the mouse pointer outside the *Open* dialog box. You should hear the chimes or other sound you have assigned to the default beep.

If you wish, you can then go back to the *Sound* dialog box and assign some sounds to other events, such as *Windows Exit*.

Finding and Playing Sounds

As your multimedia expertise grows, you are likely to build up quite a collection of sound files on your PC — including your own recordings and files that come with multimedia software. It's likely that these files will be stored in different directories. As explained below, you can use your mouse within the *Files* section of the *Sound* dialog box to navigate your way to any waveform file stored on your system. You can then test (play) the sound and, if you wish, assign it to a Windows event.

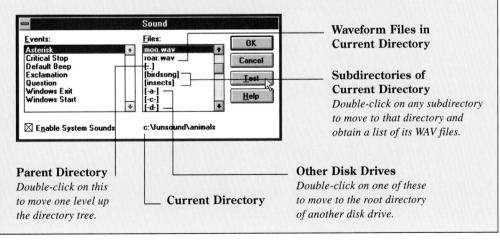

Waveform Files in Current Directory

Subdirectories of Current Directory
Double-click on any subdirectory to move to that directory and obtain a list of its WAV files.

Parent Directory
Double-click on this to move one level up the directory tree.

Current Directory

Other Disk Drives
Double-click on one of these to move to the root directory of another disk drive.

Sound Recorder

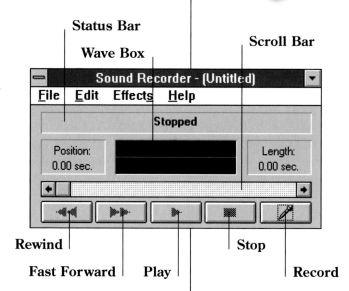

NOW THAT YOU HAVE YOUR SOUND CARD INSTALLED, it's time to try your hand at recording. The Sound Recorder utility in Windows lets you record sounds and save them to disk as WAV files. You can also use this utility to edit sounds, add special effects, and mix two sound files together. Once you have created a file, it can be imported into documents or assigned to a system event, as described on the previous page.

The Sound Recorder Window

The *Sound Recorder* icon is normally found in the *Accessories* window. Open the program by double-clicking on the icon. A small window will appear.

The buttons along the bottom of the window are used to move around in the sound file, much as you would with a tape recorder. In the center of the window is a display panel called the Wave box. The green line in the center of the Wave box represents the baseline of a sound wave. When you play a file, this display changes to show a graphic representation of the wave.

To the right of the Wave box, the *Length* box shows the total length of the sound file. The *Position* box on the left shows your position within the sound file (in seconds). Directly below the Wave box is a scroll bar for moving through the sound file.

Status Bar

Wave Box

Scroll Bar

Sound Recorder - (Untitled)

File **Edit** **Effects** **Help**

Stopped

Position: 0.00 sec.

Length: 0.00 sec.

Rewind

Stop

Fast Forward **Play** **Record**

How to Record and Save Sound

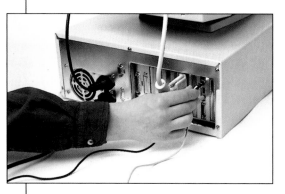

1 With your PC's power turned off, plug your microphone into the "Mic" port on the back of the sound card, and switch the microphone on (if it has a switch). Now turn on your PC and open Windows.

2 Start the Sound Recorder utility by double-clicking on the *Sound Recorder* icon in the *Accessories* window.

?

What's the Baseline?
The baseline is the green line that divides the Wave box in half horizontally. It is used to measure the wave's amplitude, or volume. The longer the distance from the baseline to the peak of a particular wave, the louder the sound that was recorded at that particular point.

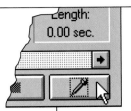

3 Click on the Record button in the *Sound Recorder* window. After a brief pause, you will see the slide on the scroll bar jump from left to right, and the position and length counters will start to increment.

4 Start speaking into the microphone; the sound waves are displayed as you speak. Note the message displayed in the status bar.

5 When you want to finish recording, click on the Stop button. The status bar will change to show that you have stopped recording, and the length of the recorded file will be displayed in the *Length* box.

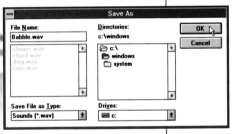

6 Select the *Save* option in the *File* menu.

7 The *Save As* dialog box will appear, with WINDOWS as the current directory. Type the name of your sound sample, **BABBLE**, into the *File Name* box. The WAV filename extension is added automatically. Click on *OK* to save the file to the WINDOWS directory.

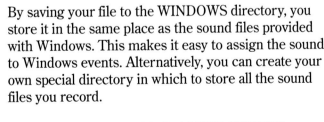

By saving your file to the WINDOWS directory, you store it in the same place as the sound files provided with Windows. This makes it easy to assign the sound to Windows events. Alternatively, you can create your own special directory in which to store all the sound files you record.

RECORDING THROUGH LINE INPUTS
If you don't feel like hearing your own voice booming out of your PC, you can record from another source — such as a stereo — using a line input. Make sure that you plug this cord into the "Line In" jack on the back of the sound card. The microphone jack is intended for low-level (unamplified) input only, and high-level input could damage the card. The other end of the cord plugs into the "Line Out" jacks on the stereo.

Stereo Line Out

PC Line In

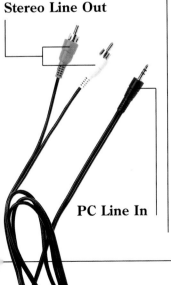

Nothing's Happening!
If you try to make a recording and no sound waves appear in the Wave box, the recording level might need to be turned up. Consult your sound card manual to see how to reset the microphone input level.
The software that comes with a sound card may include a utility (often called a mixer utility) that allows you to alter the input level.

Record Lengths
When you begin recording, the status bar will tell you for how long you can record — usually 60 seconds, although it depends on the amount of memory and free disk space available on your PC. Try not to record for more than 20 seconds or your sound file will become very big.

Playing a Sound File

Once you have recorded and saved your sound file, you will want to hear the result. Click on the Play button — the file will automatically rewind to the beginning before it starts playing. The first few seconds of the file will probably be silent; when your recording does start playing, watch the Wave box carefully and compare what you see to the quality of the sound you hear.

NAVIGATION SKILLS

Click on the Stop button at any point while the sound file is playing. Now practice using the buttons and the scroll bar to move around the file.

You have already seen that if you are at the end of the file, clicking on the Play button causes it to rewind automatically before it plays. However, if you stop the file during play or use the scroll bar to go to a particular position, clicking on the Play button will begin playing from the point shown in the Wave box.

To move to the beginning of the file, click once on the Rewind button. To move to the end, click once on the Fast Forward button.

You can also use the keyboard to get around: Pressing the Home key will move you to the beginning of the file, and pressing the End key takes you to the end.

The Scroll Arrow
Click once on a scroll arrow to move forward or backward through the file by one tenth of a second.

The Scroll Bar
Click once on the scroll bar to move forward or backward by one second.

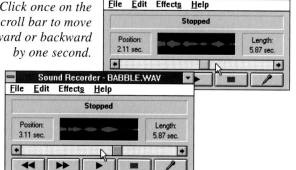

Superior Sounds
Don't be discouraged if your first attempt at recording sound is not very successful. A microphone has limits on the loudest and quietest sounds that it can record, and it takes practice to regulate your voice. If the sound is too loud, the signal will get distorted; if it is too soft, it will barely register.

USING YOUR MICROPHONE CORRECTLY
A lot of problems with distorted sound recordings are caused by incorrect use of the microphone. If you hold the microphone too close to your mouth, your recording will contain a lot of hissing and your speech will sound full of "S"s. If you hold the microphone too far away, your voice will be too faint and the recording will pick up an echo effect from the room.

The ideal distance between the microphone and your mouth varies for different microphones. However, a distance of eight inches is a good place to start experimenting.

Get It Taped
With a bit of practice you will soon be recording professional-sounding files!

Recording a New File

If you are not happy with the sound quality, you can easily move to the beginning of the file and record a new sample over the existing sound. Once you are satisfied with the sample, don't forget to save the updated file.

If you want to record a completely new file, choose *New* from the *File* menu. If you did not save your original file, a dialog box will ask if you wish to save the changes to this file before opening a new *Sound Recorder* window.

New File
Choose New *from the* File *menu to begin a new recording.*

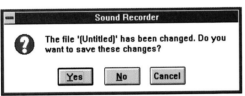

Saving Changes
If you don't save your work before starting a new file, a dialog box will give you the option to do so.

OPENING AND CLOSING FILES
To leave Sound Recorder, choose *Exit* from the *File* menu. To play or edit an existing file, choose *Open* from the *File* menu. Select the file you want from the *Open* dialog box and click on *OK*.

Not Just a Pretty Picture

The graphic depiction of the sound wave in the Wave box not only looks impressive, it also serves a purpose. By ensuring that the wave never touches the top of the Wave box, you can guard against distortion as you record. You can also check for distortion by watching the wave as you play back a file you have recorded.

Editing Sound Files

You will usually need to edit portions of the sound files you record. It's difficult to start speaking at exactly the right moment, for instance, and the first few seconds of a recording are often silent and need to be deleted. You might also want to combine two separate files into a single file, or add an echo to a voice. These and other editing tasks are easy with Sound Recorder.

Deleting the Beginning of a Sound Sample

1 Using the navigation techniques you learned on page 56, move through the sound file until the baseline in the Wave box changes to show where the sound recording begins. Stop the file at that point.

2 Choose *Delete Before Current Position* from the *Edit* menu. Sound Recorder will delete everything up to and including the segment in the Wave box.

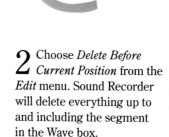

3 Confirm that you want to delete this section by clicking on *OK* in the dialog box.

4 Play the recording to check that the edit has worked properly.

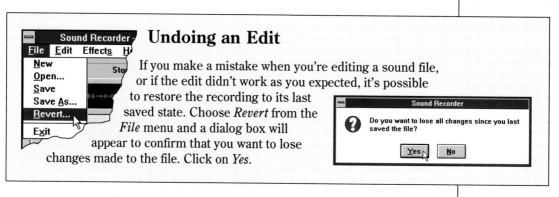

Undoing an Edit

If you make a mistake when you're editing a sound file, or if the edit didn't work as you expected, it's possible to restore the recording to its last saved state. Choose *Revert* from the *File* menu and a dialog box will appear to confirm that you want to lose changes made to the file. Click on *Yes*.

DELETING THE END OF A SOUND SAMPLE

The end of a recording often includes a knocking noise from the microphone being put down. You can delete this in the same way that you cut out the beginning.

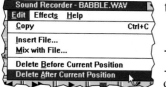

1 Move to the point in the recording at which you want the sound file to end. Choose *Delete After Current Position* from the *Edit* menu.

2 Confirm that you want to delete this section by clicking on *OK* in the dialog box. Then rewind to the beginning and play the entire file to check that your edit worked correctly.

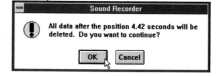

INSERTING ONE FILE INTO ANOTHER

The *Edit* menu can also be used to insert the contents of one sound file into another. For example, you can add a touch of majesty to your BABBLE.WAV file by inserting the Windows TADA.WAV file into it.

1 Open your BABBLE.WAV sound file and find the position at which you want to insert the TADA.WAV file. You might want to place it at the beginning of the file for a heraldic start! When you are at the chosen point in the file, choose *Insert File* from the *Edit* menu.

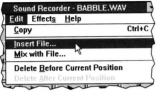

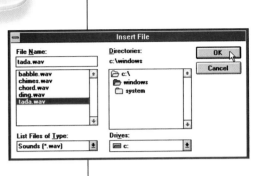

2 In the *Insert File* dialog box, choose TADA.WAV from the list under *File Name* and click on *OK*.

Saving the New File

Rewind the file to the beginning and click on the Play button to hear the whole recording. If you are happy with the result, don't forget to save the file. You have two options here: if you choose *Save* from the *File* menu (left), the original BABBLE.WAV file will be replaced by the new file. If you would prefer to keep the original BABBLE.WAV file, choose *Save As* from the *File* menu, and then give the new file a different name (right).

If you're not happy with your recording, use the *Revert* command in the *File* menu to discard the inserted file and keep the original intact.

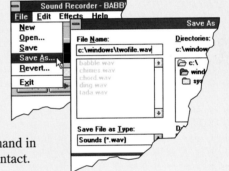

MIXING IN A SECOND SOUND

Sound Recorder also offers the option of mixing two sound files together so that they play back simultaneously. Try putting some atmosphere into your BABBLE.WAV file by mixing in a little background music. If you don't have any music files on your PC, use your microphone (or line inputs, if you have any) to record a musical sequence from your stereo.

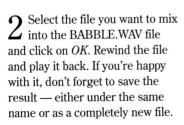

1 Move to the beginning of the BABBLE.WAV file and choose *Mix with File* from the *Edit* menu.

2 Select the file you want to mix into the BABBLE.WAV file and click on *OK*. Rewind the file and play it back. If you're happy with it, don't forget to save the result — either under the same name or as a completely new file.

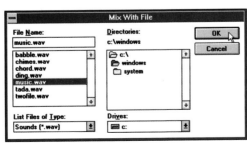

Adding Special Effects

With the aid of the Sound Recorder *Effects* menu, you can turn your simple audio files into super sounds! You can improve a recording easily by adding echo effects, changing the speed of play, changing the volume, and even playing the sound backward.

The Effects Menu in Sound Recorder

PUMPING UP THE VOLUME

When you mix two files together or insert one file into another, the ability to increase or decrease the volume of a recording is particularly useful. You might find, for instance, that when you mix a music sample into a voice file, the voice is drowned out by the music. To remedy this, you can either open the file with the voice recording and increase the volume or you can turn down the volume in the music file.

Increasing the Volume of a File

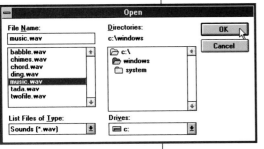

1 In Sound Recorder, open the file you want to work with.

2 Choose *Increase Volume* from the *Effects* menu. Turning up the volume of a sound file affects the whole recording, and you can only increase or decrease the level by a fixed amount (25 percent) each time.

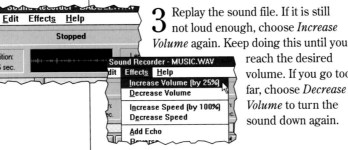

3 Replay the sound file. If it is still not loud enough, choose *Increase Volume* again. Keep doing this until you reach the desired volume. If you go too far, choose *Decrease Volume* to turn the sound down again.

DECREASING THE VOLUME OF A FILE

If you have a sound file that sounds distorted because it was recorded at too high a level (left), open the file and choose *Decrease Volume* from the *Effects* menu. Play the file and watch the Wave box to see how the signal decreased in volume (right). You should hear an improvement in the sound quality.

CHANGING THE SPEED OF A SOUND FILE

If you want to change the speed of your sound file, use one of the two options in the *Effects* menu to either increase or decrease the speed. These options only work in fixed steps: you can decrease the speed of a file by 50 percent or increase its speed by 100 percent. Remember that the sound will become a little distorted when you change the speed of the file.

RESOUNDING ECHOES

Adding an echo to a sound gives it more depth and character. If you have a voice recording that sounds a little tinny, using the *Add Echo* option often helps to make it sound more natural. *Add Echo* will add a fixed amount of echo to your whole recording.

PLAY IT BACKWARD, SAM

You can create original sounds by playing sound files backward. Experiment with different types of recordings to see what happens to different sounds when they're played backward.

Choose the *Reverse* option from the *Effects* menu to turn your sound back to front. Click on Play and you'll hear the reversed sound. If you don't like the result and you want to revert back to the original, choose *Reverse* a second time.

Compound Numbers

Once you know how to play, record, and edit Sound Recorder files, you can practice making more complex sounds. For instance, you can remix a file by making a number of copies of it, editing each copy in a different way, and then mixing the copies together for a totally new sound. For example, starting with a simple voice sound, you can produce what sounds like the chant of a thousand voices!

To copy a file, open it in Sound Recorder and choose *Save As* from the *File* menu. When the *Save As* dialog box appears, type a new name into the *File Name* box (above left). This way, the original file will be retained and you can make any number of copies to play around with (right).

Sophisticated Sounds

For more control over your finished results, try using professional sound editing software. These programs offer more options for modifying recordings than those included with Sound Recorder. For instance, an editing program might include tools for fade-in and fade-out, and the ability to cut out very specific portions of a file with a drag of the mouse.

Media Player

WINDOWS' MEDIA PLAYER IS A GENERAL-PURPOSE playback utility. You cannot use Media Player to record or create files, but you can use it to play any standard type of multimedia file — not just waveform sound files, but also MIDI, video, and animation files. You can also use Media Player to play audio CDs in your PC's CD-ROM drive.

Audio CD Player

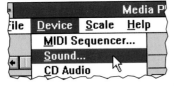

Video Player

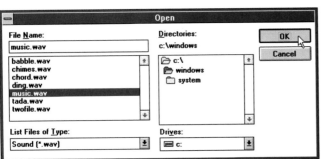

Familiar Buttons
Using Media Player is like having the controls to the above, more familiar, types of media players at your fingertips.

Using Media Player

To start Media Player, double-click on the *Accessories* group icon in Windows Program Manager. Then double-click on the *Media Player* icon in the *Accessories* window. You can use Media Player to use or control any MCI (media control interface) device on your system. MCI devices include sound cards, MIDI sequencers, audio CD-ROM drives, and packages such as Video for Windows.

Pull down Media Player's *Device* menu to see a list of the MCI devices installed. Because MCI drivers for a sound card and a MIDI sequencer are normally automatically installed when you install Windows, you should see *Sound* and *MIDI Sequencer* on this list. Other items may appear on the list, depending on the MCI devices installed on your system.

PLAYING A SOUND FILE
To start using Media Player, you must first choose the device you are going to use from the *Device* menu. If you choose a device that plays disk files, you must also specify the file you want to play.

1 Choose *Sound* from Media Player's *Device* menu.

2 An *Open* dialog box appears. The *File Name* box lists the sound files with a WAV extension in the current directory. Click on the file you want to play, and then click on *OK*.

Want to Play a MIDI Sound File?
If your sound card has a synthesizer capable of playing MIDI files, you can use Media Player to play these files. You'll find out more about MIDI in Chapter 4, but as a sample, Windows provides a MIDI file that you can play. To hear it, choose *MIDI Sequencer* from Media Player's *Device* menu. In the *Open* dialog box, choose CANYON.MID from the *File Name* box, and then click on *OK*. Back in the *Media Player* window, click on the Play button.

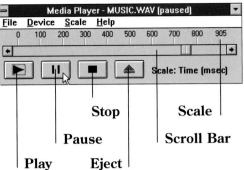

Stop

Pause

Play **Eject** **Scale** | **Scroll Bar**

3 The file is loaded and you are returned to the main *Media Player* window. You can now play, pause, or stop the file using the appropriate buttons. You can move to any point in the file using the scroll bar, scroll box, and scroll arrows. A scale above the scroll bar gives an indication of where you are in the file.

PLAYING A MUSIC CD

If you have installed a CD-ROM drive and its associated driver software on your PC (and if the drive can play music CDs), you should see *CD Audio* on Media Player's *Device* menu. If you don't, select the *Drivers* option in Windows Control Panel, and in the *Drivers* dialog box click on *Add*. In the *Add* dialog box, under *List of Drivers*, click on *[MCI] CD Audio*, and then click on *OK*. Follow the instructions to install the driver (you will need to insert one of your Windows floppy disks).

Once the driver is installed, you should see that a *CD Audio* option has appeared on Media Player's *Device* menu. You can now use Media Player to play a music CD in your CD-ROM drive.

1 Insert a music CD into your CD-ROM drive and, after starting Media Player, choose *CD Audio* from the *Device* menu.

2 Back at the main *Media Player* window, you can now play the music CD in your CD-ROM drive. If you want, you can quit Media Player and switch to some other task — the music will continue playing in the background.

Play Audio Tracks?
If you want to use Media Player to play a particular track on an audio CD, choose *Tracks* from Media Player's *Scale* menu. The scale is then divided into tracks instead of time units. Scroll to the track you want to hear and click on the Play button.

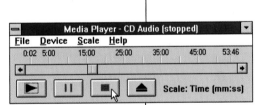

Playing Video Clips

You can also use Media Player to play video clips stored on your hard disk or on a CD-ROM, as long as a driver for video has been installed. Many multimedia titles that include video sequences (such as Microsoft *Cinemania,* or *Space Adventure* from Knowledge Adventure Inc.), as well as packages such as Microsoft's Video for Windows, install a suitable driver as part of their own setup procedure. You'll find out more about Video for Windows on page 89.

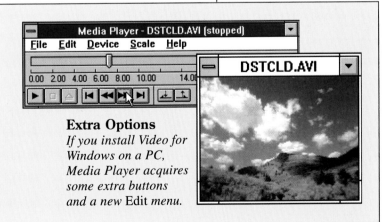

Extra Options
If you install Video for Windows on a PC, Media Player acquires some extra buttons and a new Edit *menu.*

Adding Sounds to Documents

N OW THAT YOU KNOW HOW TO RECORD and edit audio files, you can liven up your documents with the addition of some sound. Windows allows you to insert data created in one Windows application into a document created with another Windows application. This capability is called *object linking and embedding*, or *OLE*. Although we'll concentrate here on the use of OLE with sound files, OLE provides a convenient way of adding various types of media — including pictures or even video — to text-based applications. In fact, OLE provides the tools for creating a simple multimedia presentation.

Objects and Icons

An object is a collection of data — for instance, a picture file or a sound file. Objects are created in a source application and inserted into a destination document. By inserting an object using the techniques of *linking* or *embedding*, you can later edit the object from within the destination document.

Some objects (picture files, for example) can be displayed in the destination document either in their entirety or as an icon. You use a utility called Object Packager to make the choice (see page 67). Other objects (sound files, for example) can only be displayed as icons. When you double-click on the icon — which is a sort of hotspot — the object is revealed or played.

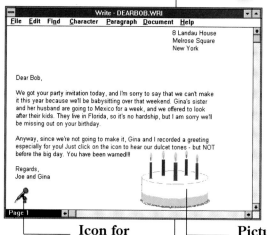

Icon for a Sound Object

Picture Object Displayed in Its Entirety

Linking and Embedding

The main difference between linking and embedding involves where the data for the object is stored.

The data for a linked object remains in the source application. The destination document itself doesn't contain the data; it only contains directions for where to find the data. If you edit a linked object, you are actually editing the original file. When you complete the edit, the original is changed, and its representation in the destination document is updated accordingly.

When you embed an object, in contrast, a copy of the data is sent to and becomes a part of the destination document. No link remains between the original data and its copy, so when you edit an embedded object, the original will remain unchanged.

Get Chatting!
Using OLE, it's easy to add a sound message to a letter created using Write, put the file on a floppy disk, and send it to a friend who can read the letter and hear your message! But make sure that your object is an embedded, not a linked object — and that your friend has a PC with a sound card!

The Information Exchange

Choosing whether to link or embed an object depends on a number of factors. Linking is useful when you want to insert an object into several documents, and anticipate that you'll want to edit the object in the future. When you edit the object, you only have to do so once — the changes will automatically appear in every document that contains links to that object. Linking is also the best choice if the size of the object file is large. The destination document stores the link rather than the object, thus keeping the size of the destination document to a minimum.

You should embed an object if you want that object always to be available in the destination document, even if the source file is removed or the destination document is moved to another PC. Note that if you want to edit any object (whether embedded or linked), the source application must be available on the PC you are using.

INSERTING A LINKED OBJECT

You can use the *Copy*, *Paste*, and *Paste Link* commands available in most Windows programs to link and embed. Windows Write supports OLE and is a good application with which to experiment. Start by linking the WAV file you created on page 55 to a Write document.

1 Open the BABBLE.WAV file in Sound Recorder and choose *Copy* from the *Edit* menu.

2 Start the Write application by double-clicking on its icon in the *Accessories* window.

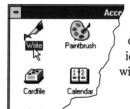

3 Maximize the *Write* window by clicking once on the Maximize button in the top right-hand corner of the window.

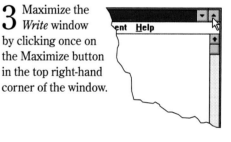

4 Type in a few lines of text, and then place the insertion point where you want to insert the sound file.

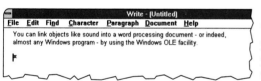

6 A microphone icon will be inserted into the Write document. Double-click on the icon with the I-beam pointer to hear the sound file.

5 Choose *Paste Link* from the *Edit* menu.

7 Choose *Save As* from the *File* menu. Type the name of the Write file in the *Save As* dialog box, and then click on *OK*.

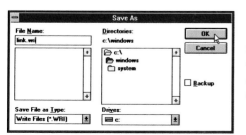

8 Leave Write by choosing *Exit* from the *File* menu.

Embedding Sound Objects

There are two ways to embed a sound object into a document. One method is to open the destination document first, then open Sound Recorder and create the object. The other method is to create the object in Sound Recorder, save it, and then import the object into the destination document.

Embedding an Object In Write

1 Create a new Write document. In the new document, move the insertion point to the place you want the sound icon to go. Choose *Insert Object* from the *Edit* menu.

2 Choose *Sound* from the displayed list and click on *OK*. The Sound Recorder utility will start. If you want to record a new sound, do so now and skip to step 5 when you have finished.

3 If you want to insert a file you recorded earlier, choose *Insert File* from the *Edit* menu.

4 Select the sound file you want to embed from the *Insert File* dialog box, and then click on *OK*.

5 Choose *Update* from the *File* menu; this will embed the sound file into your Write document.

6 A microphone icon will be inserted into the Write document (you might need to move the Sound Recorder box to see it). Choose *Exit* from the *File* menu in Sound Recorder to go back to Write.

7 Choose *Save* from the *File* menu in Write. If this is a new document, the *Save As* dialog box will appear, and you will need to name the document.

DELETING AN OBJECT

If you want to get rid of an object that is linked or embedded in a Write document, open the document and highlight the object icon. Now press the Delete key; the object and its icon will disappear.

Editing Sound Objects

Sound objects are edited in the same way, whether they are linked or embedded. However, changes made to a linked object will appear in both the original stored in the Sound Recorder application and in its representation within the destination document, whereas editing an embedded object will affect only the object in the destination document.

To see how this works, try editing the objects in the two Write documents you have just created. The steps below show how to edit the linked sound file; to edit the embedded file, follow from step 2.

Can I Edit In Sound Recorder?
Because a linked object remains in the application that created it, a linked sound file can also be edited in Sound Recorder. The changes made will automatically be reflected in the destination document.

Editing a Linked Object

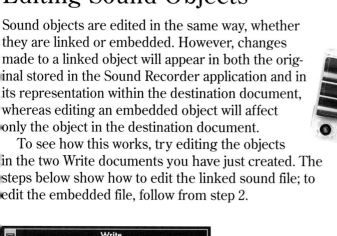

1 When you open a document that contains a linked object, a dialog box will always ask if you want to update the link. Click on *Yes*.

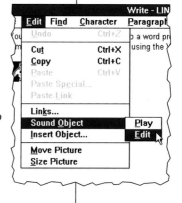

2 When the document appears, click once on the sound icon to highlight it. Choose *Sound Object* from the *Edit* menu: A submenu will appear to offer you the choice of *Play* or *Edit*. Choose *Edit*.

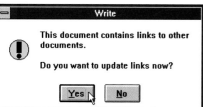

3 The *Sound Recorder* window will appear. Edit the file as you wish.

4 Choose *Exit* from the *File* menu in Sound Recorder and confirm that you want to save the changes made.

Object Packager

If you would like to choose the icon used to represent an object, use the Object Packager utility to insert an object into a document.

To use Object Packager, open a Write document and choose *Insert Object* from the *Edit* menu. Select *Package* from the menu and the *Object Packager* dialog box will open (left). Click on *Insert Icon* to see the *Insert Icon* box with its selection of icons (below). Use the scroll buttons to find an icon you want to use; when you find one, click on it to select it, and then click on *OK*.

Now choose *Import* from the *File* menu. The *Import* dialog box will open. Choose the actual object you want to insert in your Write document and click on *OK*. Now exit Object Packager. You will be prompted to update the object; click on *Yes*. The icon you chose will appear in the Write document. Double-click on this to hear (or see) the object you imported.

4

CHAPTER FOUR

Getting Adventurous

*In this chapter, you'll look at other
types of media that can form part of your
multimedia experiments. MIDI sound files, pictures,
video, and animation can all enhance your multimedia
presentations. You'll find out about the hardware and
software you need to create and work with MIDI background music, photographs, drawings, short video
sequences, and cartoons. In Chapter 5, you'll find
out how you can link all these together with
text and waveform sound files to build
a multimedia project or presentation.*

THE WORLD OF MIDI • PICTURE THIS
MAKING MOVIES • GET ANIMATED

The World of MIDI

I N CHAPTER 3, YOU FOUND OUT HOW TO record, edit, and play digital audio (waveform) files. Waveform files have an important place in the world of multimedia, but they're not the only type of sound file you can create and manipulate on a computer. If you want to experiment with the more sophisticated sound capabilities of your multimedia PC — and particularly if you have musical inclinations — you'll need to know about MIDI.

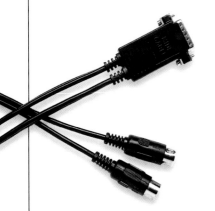

MIDI Connector Cables

What Is MIDI?

MIDI (musical instrument digital interface) is a protocol that governs the exchange of data between electronic musical instruments and computers. Unlike a waveform sound file, which contains digitized audio that a sound card plays directly, a MIDI file contains instructions for playing notes. These instructions are sent to a *synthesizer* and control each note's pitch, the timing and duration of the notes, and so on. MIDI instructions can be sent over several channels — much like a CB radio — allowing several of the synthesizer's instruments to be played simultaneously.

Small Is Beautiful!
Because MIDI files store MIDI instructions rather than digitized waveforms, they are much smaller than waveform files — usually less than 1 percent of the size for the same playing time.

Playing a MIDI File

To be heard, a MIDI file has to be fed into a piece of hardware called a synthesizer, which translates the instructions in the file into notes that are then output by the synthesizer as music through speakers.

Synthesizers
Synthesizers vary in their quality and sophistication, but all are capable of creating a variety of instrument sounds. So when you play a MIDI file through a synthesizer, you can choose what each track should sound like — for example, like a piano, a guitar, or a glockenspiel.

MIDI Message
The instructions in a MIDI file are encoded in digital form, as in any other computer file.

Synthesizer on Sound Card

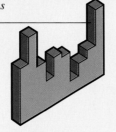

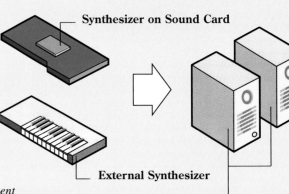

Disk
A MIDI file may be stored on a hard disk, a floppy disk, or a CD-ROM disc.

Alternative Routes
The messages in a MIDI file can be sent either to a synthesizer on a sound card or to an external synthesizer connected to your PC. An external synthesizer may be connected either to the MIDI port on your sound card or to a special MIDI interface card.

External Synthesizer

Speakers

HOW MIDI FILES ARE CREATED

To create MIDI music on a PC, you need to install a piece of software called a *MIDI sequencer*. A sequencer can be used to record, edit, and play MIDI files.

To start recording a MIDI file, you connect an electronic instrument that supports MIDI — like a MIDI keyboard or guitar — via a cable to the MIDI port at the back of a sound card or to a *MIDI interface card*. You then run the sequencer program. As you play notes on the instrument, the sequencer software records your actions. Most sequencers allow you to select how the recorded notes are displayed — traditional tabulature for those who read music, or a grid-like display for those who don't.

MIDI Instruments
Various instruments can be used for recording MIDI, but a keyboard is the most common. If the keyboard has a built-in synthesizer, it can also be used to play the MIDI file.

Get Some Advice!
Although recording MIDI music can be quite straightforward, try experimenting with existing MIDI files first (see page 72) — and get help from an experienced source before you buy a MIDI instrument or synthesizer.

MIDI Cable

Sequencer Program Displayed on Screen

Screen from Cakewalk Professional for Windows (Twelve Tone Systems) — a MIDI Sequencer

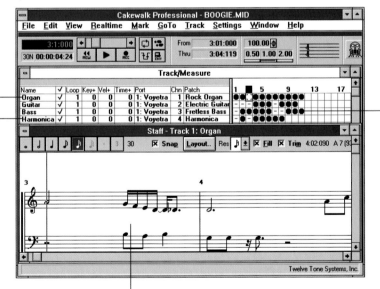

Recorded Tracks

Measure Pane
Each square represents a measure (musical interval) on a track. A filled square indicates that there is a musical event in that measure on that track.

Choose Your Instrument?
Remember that, when you play a MIDI file, you can assign each track to any of several instrument sounds. You're not restricted to the instruments used to record the file. For example, a three-track MIDI file recorded with a keyboard could be played back to sound like a grand piano, bass guitar, and flute.

A Note of Your Actions
As you record each track, your actions are stored by the sequencer and can be displayed in various formats. Here the notes on a track are displayed using a conventional musical staff. You can also use this window to compose music directly on the screen by placing notes on the staff with a mouse — though this is likely to appeal only to accomplished composers!

How Can I Use MIDI?

As you develop your interest in multimedia, there are different levels at which you can get involved in MIDI — depending on your musical inclinations and your budget.

SOUND CARD ONLY

If your sound card contains a built-in synthesizer — as most sound cards sold nowadays do — you can use it to play MIDI files. Many music-based multimedia products (such as Music Technology Associates' *Music Mentor* and Microsoft's *Multimedia Beethoven: The Ninth Symphony*) contain MIDI files that you can listen to. MIDI samples are also available from electronic bulletin boards such as CompuServe and you can also purchase them in commercial packages or as shareware files. Many sound cards come with a collection of sample MIDI files.

You can also use Windows Media Player (see page 62) to play any MIDI file from your hard disk or a CD-ROM. You can insert a MIDI file as an embedded object into another file, such as a Write document, and you can incorporate MIDI files into multimedia presentations (subject to copyright restrictions).

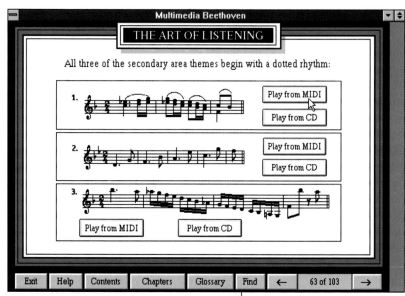

Click and Listen
With an interactive product such as Multimedia Beethoven, *hearing MIDI music is simply a question of clicking on the appropriate button on the screen.*

Synthesizers on Sound Cards

The synthesizers on sound cards differ in the way they create sounds, and this affects the quality of the MIDI sounds produced. Lower-end synthesizers generate sounds using mathematical formulas (FM synthesis). Unfortunately, FM-synthesized sounds only approximate the sounds of real instruments and have a characteristic digital "color."

Other synthesizers use short digital recordings of actual instruments (sampled sounds). These provide much more realistic sounds, but sound cards that carry this type of synthesizer (such as the MultiSound card from Turtle Beach Systems) are pricier. Some cards, such as the Roland SCC-1, *only* support MIDI sounds and do not support the recording or playing of waveform files.

Synthesizer Chip

Base or Extended?
The synthesizers on sound cards differ in the number of instrument sounds and notes they can play at one time. A base-level synthesizer supports three melodic instrument parts and can play six notes simultaneously. An extended-level synthesizer supports nine melodic instruments and can play 16 notes simultaneously. Most FM-based sound cards are base-level devices, whereas most sample-based sound cards are extended-level devices.

ADDING A SEQUENCER

The next level up in experimenting with MIDI involves installing and using a sequencer program on your PC. Windows does not provide a MIDI sequencer. However, some sound cards and multimedia upgrade kits that support MIDI come bundled with sequencer software. Alternatively, a wide range of sequencer software is available as shareware or commercially.

With a MIDI-equipped sound card and a sequencer, you can edit existing MIDI files, experiment using different instruments for the different tracks in a file, and play back your arrangements through the synthesizer on your sound card. You can also create musical scores from scratch.

ADDING EXTERNAL DEVICES

The most sophisticated way to use MIDI involves connecting one or more external *MIDI devices* to your PC — instruments for recording sounds, and synthesizers for playing them back. Often the input instrument and the synthesizer are incorporated into one unit, such as a synthesizer with a keyboard controller attached, or a drum machine.

External synthesizers vary from reasonably priced to very expensive. One of the advantages of an external synthesizer is that it has many controls that allow you to define and create completely new sounds. These sound definitions can be saved on your PC using MIDI control codes. You can build up a library of sound definitions and download each one to the synthesizer when you need to use it.

Sequence It?
The screen above is from a sequencer called Midisoft Recording Session. This sequencer includes many sample MIDI files you can experiment with.

Rock On
Many pop and rock bands create portions of their music with MIDI instruments, recording all the notes into a MIDI sequencer. These MIDI files can then be output while the musicians record live vocals and additional instrumental tracks, which can then all be mixed together.

Connecting Devices

You connect an external MIDI device to a sound card or to a MIDI interface card in your PC via a cable. Most sound cards have a single MIDI port (near right), but MIDI interface cards and some sound cards (far right) have separate In and Out ports. Similarly, an external device such as a keyboard synthesizer has In and Out ports. The appropriate connections are as shown.

The connection between your PC and the Out port on a keyboard synthesizer allows you to record actions played on the keyboard. The connection between your PC and the In port on a synthesizer allows you to output MIDI files from the PC to the synthesizer.

MIDI devices may also have a Thru port. This relays anything received on that device's In port to another device. The arrangement at far right, for example, would allow you to output a rhythm track from your PC to a drum machine while you played and recorded a melody track using the keyboard.

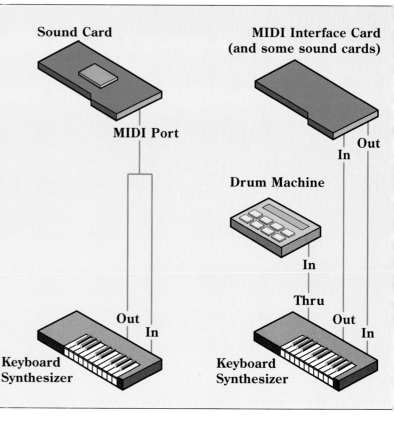

A Closer Look at Sequencers

MIDI sequencers vary in their sophistication and their interface with the user, but most offer a host of features and tools that allow you to analyze and manipulate every aspect of a MIDI file. The screens below and on the next page, from two sequencers called WinJammer and Cakewalk Professional for Windows, show some typical features.

Record, Play, Rewind, and Fast Forward Buttons

Menu Bar

Tempo Adjustment
You can vary the tempo (the speed at which it plays) of a whole MIDI file.

Track Window
The tracks in a file are all listed, together with the channel and patch number assigned to each (see "Tracks, Channels, and Patch Numbers" on page 76).

Piano Roll Notation
This window uses marks on a grid to indicate the notes on a track and their durations. You can easily remove or add notes in this window.

Event List
Most sequencers offer a list of all the notes on a particular track, with each note's timing and duration.

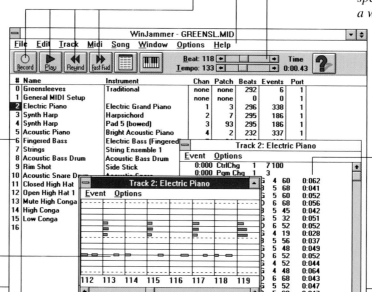

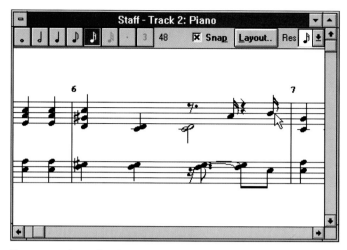

Rearranging the Notes
This staff notation window is taken from Cakewalk Professional for Windows. Using your mouse, you can easily add or delete notes from the score, change their duration, move them around, and so on.

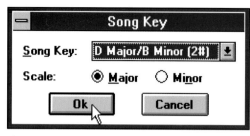

Change the Key
The Song Key *dialog box in WinJammer allows you to change the key of a whole MIDI file, for example, from C major to D major, or between a major and minor key.*

On the Beat
Some sequencers allow you to "quantize" a file. Quantizing smoothes out any timing quirks and forces the rhythm onto the beat.

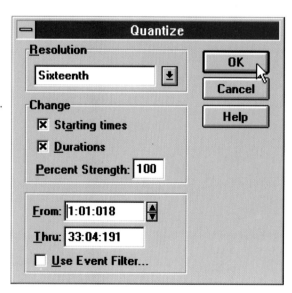

CONFIGURING A SEQUENCER

You may have to configure a sequencer for use with a sound card or a MIDI interface. You must define an input port if you want to record using the sequencer, and an output port if you want to play MIDI files. To configure a sequencer, you normally have to access a dialog box, such as the one shown below, in which the available ports are listed. These ports are equivalent to device drivers that are usually installed when you install your sound card or MIDI interface card. If no ports are available, or if the available ports don't seem to work, try using the *Drivers* option in Windows Control Panel to install a MIDI driver from the floppy disk supplied with the card.

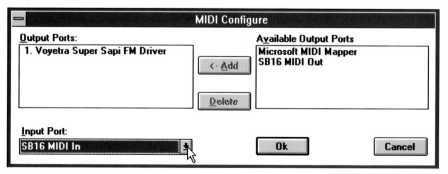

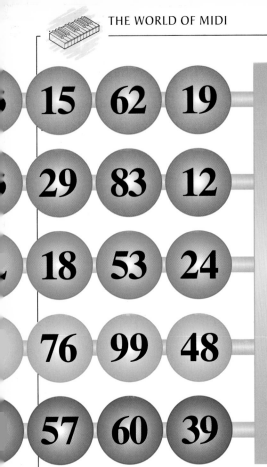

Tracks, Channels, and Patch Numbers

When a MIDI file is sent from your PC to a synthesizer, each track must be assigned to a specific *channel*. Standard MIDI uses 16 channels, but not all synthesizers can handle that many channels. It's possible to assign different MIDI channels to different hardware devices — for example, you could assign channels 13 through 16 to the synthesizer on a sound card and other channels to an external device (see "The MIDI Mapper" on the next page).

Each channel also has a *patch* mapped to it. A patch is MIDI jargon for a specific set of instrument sounds. This information tells a synthesizer which of the different instrument sounds (programs) it offers should be used for that channel. Synthesizers vary in the sounds they can produce. To prevent confusion, a General MIDI standard has been set up that defines program numbers (patches) for 128 different instruments and other sounds. For example, violin is program number 40, oboe is number 68, and so on. The General MIDI standard also defines 46 drum sounds.

By using devices that conform to the General MIDI standard, you can ensure that a MIDI file set up to play piano and bass on one synthesizer doesn't come out sounding like guitar and flute on another synthesizer.

Birds and Helicopters

The General MIDI standard includes program numbers for sounds such as bird-tweets and the sounds of the seashore, helicopters, applause, gunshots, and breathing. You can build these sounds into your MIDI files and hear them played through any synthesizer that supports the full range of General MIDI sounds.

Channel to Channel

The channel and patch are defined for each track in a MIDI file. For example, track 2 loaded into the sequencer at right is assigned to channel 1 and to the honky-tonk piano patch (program number 3 in the General MIDI standard). Using the sequencer, you can easily change the patch assigned to each track, making it easy to experiment with different instrument combinations.

Cakewalk Professional - WYSIWYG.MID* - [Track/Measure]

File Edit View Realtime Mark GoTo Track Settings Window Help

	Name	✓	Loop	Key+	Vel+	Time+	Port	Chn	Patch	Vol	Pan	Size
1	General MIDI	m	1	0	0	0	1: Voyetra	--	-none-	---	---	0
2	Piano	✓	1	0	0	0	1: Voyetra	1	Honky-tonk Pian	80	---	1691
3	Bass	✓	1	0	0	0	1: Voyetra	2	Fretless Bass	80	---	590
4	Organ	✓	1	0	0	0	1: Voyetra	3	Hammond Organ	100	---	566
5	Guitar	✓	1	0	0	0	1: Voyetra	4	Electric Guitar (	100	---	474
6	Marimba	✓	1	0	0	0	1: Voyetra	5	Marimba	80	---	189
7	Violin	✓	1	0	0	0	1: Voyetra	6	Violin	85	---	209
8	Trumpet	✓	1	0	0	0	1: Voyetra	7	Trumpet	80	---	6
9	Xylophone	✓	1	0	0	0	1: Voyetra	8	Xylophone	80	---	436
10	Horn	✓	1	0	0	0	1: Voyetra	9	French Horn	80	---	9
11	Ooohs	✓	1	0	0	0	1: Voyetra	10	-none-	80	---	100
12	Drums	✓	1	0	0	0	1: Voyetra	10	-none-	80	---	4
13	Drums	✓	1	0	0	0	1: Voyetra	10	-none-	80	---	7
14	Drums	✓	1	0	0	0	1: Voyetra	10	-none-	80	---	4
15	Drums	✓	1	0	0	0	1: Voyetra	10	-none-	80	---	12
16												
17												
18												
19												
20												
21												
22												
23												
24												
25												

15:1:000 From 9:01:000 144.00
30N 00:00:23:10 Thru 9:04:191 0.50 1.00 2.00

Twelve Tone Systems, Inc.

The MIDI Mapper

The MIDI Mapper is a utility provided by Windows for remapping the channel and patch identification numbers in MIDI files. If a synthesizer supports General MIDI, you can assume it will play General MIDI files properly, and you should not need to use the MIDI Mapper. If, however, you connect a synthesizer that does not support General MIDI to your PC, you can use the MIDI Mapper to remap the channels and patch numbers in a MIDI file for use by that synthesizer. The MIDI Mapper can also be used for playing, on a General MIDI device, a MIDI file that was created on a nonstandard instrument.

Which Channels to Use?

A base-level synthesizer uses channels 13 through 15 for melodic instruments and channel 16 for percussion. An extended-level synthesizer uses channels 1 through 9 for melodic instruments and channel 10 for percussion.

Accessing the MIDI Mapper
The MIDI Mapper is accessed by double-clicking on the MIDI Mapper icon in Windows Control Panel.

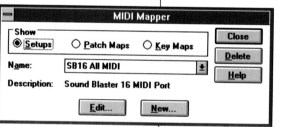

MIDI Mapper Dialog Box
With the Setups button selected, you can choose from a variety of setups for different synthesizers by dropping down the Name list. If the synthesizer you wish to use is not listed, you must create your own setup.

Patch Map Dialog Box
Creating a new setup involves first creating a key map (to reassign the numbers used for percussion sounds), then a patch map (to assign the numbers used to identify instrument sounds and their volumes), and finally a channel map (to determine which channels should go to which devices). Shown at right is the dialog box used to define patch mappings. The synthesizer manual should provide a guide to the required mappings.

Go Carefully!
The MIDI Mapper is a sophisticated tool, and using it to specify MIDI settings can be complicated. Unless you are already knowledgeable about MIDI, stay clear of the MIDI Mapper or get help from an expert when using it.

MIDI Patch Map: 'MT32'

1 based patches

Src Patch	Src Patch Name	Dest Patch	Volume %	Key Map Name
0	Acoustic Grand Piano	0	100	[None]
1	Bright Acoustic Piano	1	100	[None]
2	Electric Grand Piano	3	100	[None]
3	Honky-tonk Piano	7	100	[None]
4	Rhodes Piano	5	100	[None]
5	Chorused Piano	6	100	[None]
6	Harpsichord	17	100	[None]
7	Clavinet	21	100	[None]
8	Celesta	22	100	[None]
9	Glockenspiel	101	100	[None]
10	Music Box	101	100	[None]
11	Vibraphone	98	100	[None]
12	Marimba	104	100	[None]
13	Xylophone	103	100	[None]
14	Tubular Bells	102	100	[None]
15	Dulcimer	105	100	[None]

OK   **Cancel**   **Help**

Picture This

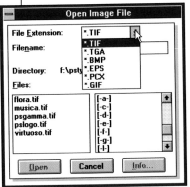

NOW THAT YOU KNOW ALL ABOUT sound, let's take a look at graphics. You need pictures to experiment with multimedia creation, and there are a number of ways to get them. You can create your own using a paint program, you can choose them from a disk containing pre-drawn images, or you can digitize your own photographs using a scanner and then import them into your PC. Before you choose and use graphics, however, you need to understand about image *file formats*.

Image File Formats

As with any other data, when you save an image to disk, it is stored in a file. Different software programs use different formats for storing graphics files, and you can identify the format a graphic uses by its filename extension (for example, PCX, TIF, or BMP). These days, most software programs support many different formats.

The format used to store a graphic determines a lot about the image itself — for instance, its size and the number of colors it can contain. Knowing something about file formats will help you choose the best images to use in your multimedia creations.

The first thing to understand is that, although there are several formats, images always fall into one of two categories — *bitmap* or *vector*.

Opening Images
When you import an image into a program like Photostyler (above), you need to specify the file extension.

Bitmap Images

Bitmap images (like the picture from *Microsoft Dinosaurs* at left) are made up of individual dots called pixels. The image file stores information about each pixel, including its location and color. Each pixel is the same size, and the number of pixels in an image determines its quality: the more pixels, the sharper the image. High resolution bitmap images require a lot of disk storage space and take longer to appear on screen than low resolution images.

Vector Images

Vector files contain descriptions of the shapes and colors that make up an image. A square, for instance, would be described in terms of the area it covers, the length and thickness of its lines, and so on; to display the square, the software converts the description to shapes and colors. In the vector image on the left (from Applied Optical Media's *The Animals Encyclopedia*) the bird is described in terms of the lines, shapes, and colors that make up its image.

Jagged Edges
The more you increase the size of a bitmap image, the more you can see the pixels that make up the image.

A 4-Bit Color Image

DIFFERENT STROKES
Bitmap and vector formats each have certain advantages and disadvantages.

The bitmap format is very good at maintaining an illusion of gradual color transition, and this makes it the best choice for photographs and realistic images. The disadvantage of bitmapped pictures is that, when you enlarge them, each individual pixel is enlarged, and the picture loses quality because of jagged edges.

Vector images are composed of mathematically described lines and shapes, so they can be enlarged or stretched without fear of creating jagged edges. The drawback to vector images is that, although they are good at color reproduction, they are not good at fine detail or at reproducing gradual color transitions.

Painting By Number

Another description you might come across in image files relates to the number of colors available to each pixel. If an image is described as 4-bit, it means that each pixel can be one of 16 colors; if an image is 8-bit, there are 256 colors available to each pixel. In a 24-bit image, each pixel can be one of 16.77 million colors. The more colors, the smoother the color transitions in an image, and the less obvious the pixels.

The number of colors you can see on your screen also depends on the monitor and display adapter on your PC (see "Pixels and Colors" on page 47).

Line Description
Vector images are made up of lines that can be enlarged without any loss of picture quality.

An 8-Bit Color Image

Choosing a Format

There are many types of graphics file formats. Some are used to store bitmap images, and others are used for vector images. A few can be used to store either. Not all software can recognize every file format, so if you import pictures to use in your documents, you must ensure that they are in a format that your software recognizes. Here are some of the more common bitmap formats:

Windows Bitmap (BMP) and Device-Independent Bitmap (DIB) Formats
The standard bitmap format used by Windows is Windows Bitmap. Files stored in this format usually have a BMP extension, although you might also come across the DIB extension (for device-independent bitmap). BMP and DIB files can store monochrome and color pictures, but not gray-scale images.

Tagged Image File Format (TIFF)
The most common format for scanned pictures is the tagged image file format (TIFF). TIFF files have a TIF filename extension. This format can store high-resolution gray-scale and color bitmap images, but files need a lot of storage space.

PCX
PCX files can handle gray-scale and color bitmap images, and they are more space-efficient than TIFF files. This format is supported by most applications.

What's a Gray Scale?
In *gray-scale* images, each pixel can be one of a number of levels of gray (unlike monochrome, in which each pixel is either black or white). See page 84 for more on gray scales.

Visual Sources

Now that you know a little about graphics file formats, you can investigate various picture sources to find exactly what you're looking for. Pictures can be used with sound and text files to create simple multimedia projects; not only are they attractive to the eye, they are also a highly effective form of communication.

CLIP ART

Many software companies produce *clip art* libraries. Clip art collections consist of pictures on floppy disk or CD-ROM disc that you can copy into your documents. Clip art images might include an assortment of drawings, photographs, diagrams, and maps, or they might concentrate on a specific type of image, like digitized photographs.

Some clip art libraries offer a wide range of pictures, including presentation art (pointers, borders, backgrounds), medical art (parts of the body), and even cartoon characters. Others concentrate on specific topics, like cityscapes or insects. The images usually come with a license for unlimited use, although you would be wise to study the copyright notice carefully.

Once you have copied the image you want to use onto a hard or floppy disk, you can use an editing program to change the picture to your liking (see "Image Editing" on page 85).

Clip Art Collections
The top four vector images shown above are included with the presentation program Microsoft PowerPoint. Below these are two bitmapped images from Corel's North American Wildlife, a collection of clip art on CD-ROM disc.

SCANNED IMAGES

Scanners can be used to translate a printed picture into an electronic format that your PC will recognize. Scanners work like photocopiers, except that instead of producing a paper copy of an image, scanners convert pictures to a digital format that can be saved to a hard or floppy disk. If you don't have your own scanner, you can use a commercial service bureau to scan the image for you (see page 83 for more on scanners).

CREATING YOUR OWN IMAGES

If you can't find the right clip art or picture to scan, you can always draw it yourself — whatever you have in mind, you'll find a program that will help you create it. Before buying a drawing package, however, think carefully about what you want it to do. The variety of programs available is as broad as their price range, and there's no point in buying a complex, expensive program when your requirements are simple.

Image-creation software can be broadly divided into three categories: paint programs, design programs, and image editing programs.

Packaged Pictures
Some software packages, like graphics programs, come with a collection of clip art. If you are in the market for this type of application, check to see if it offers clip art. Be careful, though: the images might be of the simple black-and-white variety that is more suited to desktop publishing than to multimedia.

Picking a Package

Paint programs let you create bitmap images. Features vary between programs, but most let you draw or paint using media and methods that parallel traditional art techniques, such as using different sizes of brushes or pencils. Shapes can be filled with a color from a color palette that you can customize, and you can usually cut out parts of an image, paste bits in another place, distort and rotate areas, and erase.

Design packages tend to be vector-based and are used to draw objects rather than to paint pictures. They are good for technical drawings, and the more powerful programs can be used to design complex 3-D images.

Image editing software is similar to paint software, only it has more features (see page 85 for more on image editing).

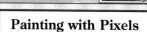

Painting with Pixels
With Fractal Design Painter, you can produce paintings that look like they have been created with natural materials.

Skewed Views
This simulation of perspectives was created with a design package called Autodesk 3D Studio.

Drawing an Image

You can familiarize yourself with paint programs by using the Paintbrush program supplied with Windows. This bitmap paint program is found in the *Accessories* window: double-click on the program's icon to open it.

On the left of the *Paintbrush* window you will find the toolbox, with the Brush tool already selected. Use this tool to draw the outline of a simple image by dragging with the mouse, and then use the Paint Roller to fill enclosed areas of the image with color. The Windows manual explains in detail how each tool is used.

Eraser
You can rub out mistakes with the Eraser tool.

Paint Roller
Once you have drawn an outline, fill the enclosed area with the Paint Roller tool.

Brush
Use this tool to paint your image.

Foreground Color
Reflects your choice from the color palette.

Background Color

Color Palette
To select the color you want to use, click on one of these colors.

Importing an Image

Once you have finished painting your picture, choose *Save As* from the *File* menu. Give the picture a name and save it as a PCX or BMP file; this will allow you to import it into most Windows applications.

Like sound files, images can be linked or embedded in a document. To embed the picture you have just created, exit Paintbrush and then open a Windows document (the example below uses Write). Position the insertion point at the place you want the picture to appear, and follow these steps:

Embedding an Image into a Write Document

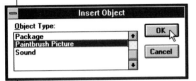

1 Choose *Insert Object* from the *Edit* menu, and then choose *Paintbrush Picture* from the *Insert Object* dialog box. Click on *OK*.

2 The *Paintbrush* window will open. Choose *Paste From* in the *Edit* menu and, when the *Paste From* dialog box appears, select the name of the file you want. Click on *OK*.

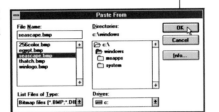

3 The image you want to embed will appear in the window. Choose *Update* from the *File* menu.

4 Choose *Exit & Return to...* from the *File* menu. You will be returned to the Write document. If you cannot see your picture in the document, use the arrows on the right to scroll upward. It will soon appear.

LINKING PICTURES

To link (rather than embed) a picture to a document, open the picture in Paintbrush and select the Pick tool (see left). The Pick tool takes the form of a crosshair; position the crosshair in the top left-hand corner of the picture. Hold down the left mouse button. Now drag the crosshair to the bottom right of the picture. As you drag, the selected area is outlined with a dotted line (see right).

When the picture is selected, choose *Copy* from the *Edit* menu. The image will be copied to the Clipboard. Now open the document you want to link the picture to, position the insertion point at the correct place, and choose *Paste Link* from the *Edit* menu.

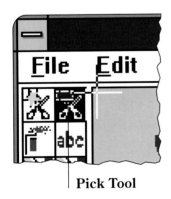

Pick Tool

Change to an Icon!
When you insert an image into a document, the picture will appear in its entirety. If you would prefer the picture to be represented by an icon, refer to "Object Packager" on page 67. Object Packager lets you select an icon to indicate the presence of an image. Double-clicking on the icon will open the picture file.

The Selected Area

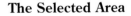

Scanners

Scanners convert printed pictures (such as photographs) into bitmap images that you can use on your PC. Some scanners let you scan images in color, whereas others offer only black-and-white facilities.

Like a copy machine, a scanner has a light-sensitive element that moves across an image and reproduces the picture. The image appears on your monitor, from which it can be saved to disk. There are two main types of scanners — handheld and desktop — and both types connect to a PC via an interface card (see page 36 for more on interface cards).

HANDHELD SCANNERS

Handheld scanners are held in the hand and physically moved over the image you want to digitize. They are smaller and cheaper than desktop devices but are more awkward to use.

Most handheld scanners are too narrow to scan a large picture in one pass — you have to scan separate strips, which are then put together by scanning software to form the image. So although handheld scanners are good at scanning small logos and simple line art, if you want to scan anything larger or more complex, a desktop machine would be a better buy.

DESKTOP SCANNERS

Desktop scanners (also called flatbed scanners) are more expensive than handheld scanners, but they are more accurate and easier to use. If you wobble as you roll a handheld scanner over a picture, the image might be distorted. Desktop scanners eliminate the need for a steady hand!

Simpler Scans
Desktop scanners are easier to use.

Hold Steady
Handheld scanners require a steady hand.

Scanner Software

All scanners come with software that controls the scanning process. The controls available depend on the type of scanner you buy, but you are usually able to adjust the brightness and contrast of an image, reduce or increase its size, and choose the scanning resolution. Some scanners also come with drawing and image manipulation software.

Desktop scanner software should let you view a rough image of the picture on your monitor before you actually scan it. This *prescan* lets you check that the picture is the right way up and aligned correctly. You should also be able to mark a crop region to define the area that you want to scan. If you don't, the entire image area will be scanned, resulting in a file much larger than you really need.

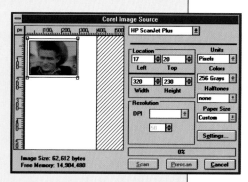

Soft Tones
Although an image scanned at 150 dpi (top) looks slightly rough when printed, it looks as smooth as the 300 dpi image (bottom) when viewed on screen.

What About Text?
If you want to scan text, you need an *optical character recognition* (*OCR*) program. OCR software recognizes text and saves it in a format that you can edit. If the original text is clear and uses a common typeface, the OCR software should easily be able to convert it to a text file. If you try to convert a poor quality fax, or text printed in an unusual font, you will have to train the OCR software to recognize each character of the alphabet for that text.

A Little Light Reading

A scanner works by reading dots of light that reflect off the picture as it scans. The more dots it reads per linear inch of picture, the higher the resolution (detail) of the scanned image. Resolutions range from 75 to 1,200 dots per inch (*dpi*). While images destined to be printed benefit from high resolutions, a resolution of 150 dpi is more than adequate for pictures that will only appear on screen at around their original size. If you need to enlarge an image on screen, a higher resolution will result in a smoother appearance.

Of course, there is the usual trade-off between image quality and file size. If an image scanned at 150 dpi takes up 300 KB of disk space, the file will grow to 600 KB if the scanning resolution is doubled to a resolution of 300 dpi.

Shades of Gray and Color

All scanners can digitize pictures into line art (stark black and white) and halftones (black and white dots that can give the appearance of gray). There is usually also a choice in the number of gray shades (called a gray scale) that a scanner can recognize.

An 8-bit monochrome scanner can detect 256 different shades of gray, and a 16-bit device can detect more than 65,000 different shades. As you increase the number of shades, the size of the image file grows.

These days, color scanners don't cost much more than black-and-white scanners. High-quality color scanners normally use 24 bits to store the color information for each pixel, which allows up to 16.77 million colors. This does result in a large image file, but a scanned picture can always be converted to 256 colors in an image editing program, where you have control over the colors used to make the change.

Take It to a Bureau!
If you want to have only a few pictures scanned — perhaps a logo or a special photograph — you can use an image bureau. These companies will scan your picture and give the digitized image back to you on a floppy disk.

Line Art

256 Gray Scale

24-Bit Color

The PhotoCD Alternative

Another way of digitizing pictures is to use a *PhotoCD* system. Originally developed by Kodak, PhotoCD is a method of storing photographs on a CD-ROM disc. Slides and negatives can also be digitized for storage on a disc. If you have a PhotoCD-compatible CD-ROM drive, the photographs can be imported into your documents (see "Multisession Capabilities" on page 35 for more information on PhotoCD-compatible drives). Many image bureaus offer a PhotoCD service.

Image Editing

Once you have an image on disk, you can use an image editing program to edit or enhance it. Image editing packages are similar to paint programs except that they include special tools for retouching and enhancing scanned images and photographs.

As with paint software, you can edit images pixel by pixel. Editing tools obviously vary between programs, but you can usually get rid of blemishes, delete unwanted portions of a picture, add textures, and change colors. Many programs also let you convert a photograph or other image into a pastiche of a painting style like impressionism.

Earthrise
Cut and Paste tools can be used to create unusual images. Open two images and you can copy portions of one picture into the other.

Clean-Shaven
The CorelPHOTO-PAINT! image editing module included in Corel-DRAW! provides a number of tools for deleting parts of an image and replacing those parts with the background. You can also change colors pixel by pixel with a customizable color palette.

Clear Views
If a picture didn't scan as well as you'd hoped, you can usually adjust the sharpness and contrast with an image editing program. The Gray/Color Correction *option in Aldus PhotoStyler, for instance, lets you enhance specific areas of an image.*

Copy Cat
Most programs let you copy areas of a picture for reproduction elsewhere. Blending tools help smooth the transition.

Making Movies

I F YOU ARE FEELING VERY ADVENTUROUS, you might want to use video in your multimedia experiments. By installing a special *video capture* card in your PC, you can display full-motion video on your monitor and then capture still images or video sequences and save them to disk.

Video in Multimedia

Video, like movie film, is made up of a series of frames of slightly different images which, when shown in rapid succession, give the impression of movement. You can use individually captured frames for multimedia projects just like other image files. Video sequences are more complicated to capture and are greedy for disk space, but they can add an extra dimension to multimedia documents or presentations.

INSTALLING A VIDEO CAPTURE CARD

Whether you want to capture single frames or video sequences, you first need to install a video capture card in your PC. Many affordable cards are available — some examples include the Video Blaster board from Creative Labs and the Bravado board from Truevision. You install a video capture card in an expansion slot in your PC in much the same way that you install a sound card (see pages 26 to 28).

How Do Capture Cards Work?

A video capture card must capture each video frame in $\frac{1}{30}$ second, before the next frame arrives. To achieve this, the card uses high-speed memory to store the captured image as a bitmap. Controlling software then transfers the bitmap to permanent storage on your hard disk.

Livening Up a Document with Video

One way to capture video sequences is to use *Video for Windows* in conjunction with a video capture card (you'll find a description of this technique on pages 89 to 91). Video for Windows saves a captured sequence as a file in a format called AVI. You can insert AVI files into Windows documents. For example, you might insert an AVI clip saved on your hard disk into a Word for Windows document and then display the document on screen as a multimedia "memo."

To do this, you first open Windows Media Player (see page 62), use the *Open* command and dialog box to display the AVI clip, and then choose *Copy Object* from Media Player's *Edit* menu. You then open Word for Windows, compose your document, position the insertion point where you want the video clip to appear, and choose *Paste* from the *Edit* menu. The clip appears as an object in the document and can be played by double-clicking on it.

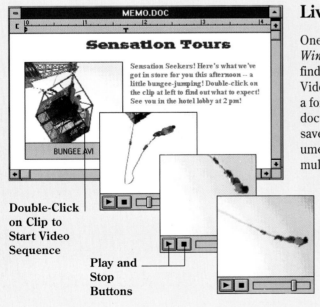

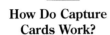

Double-Click on Clip to Start Video Sequence

Play and Stop Buttons

Single Frame Capture

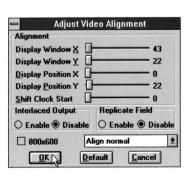

Once you've installed a video capture card, follow any further instructions that come with the card's manual. You may need to connect the card to the display adapter card (video card) in your PC. You will also need to install the device drivers and other software supplied with the card, and you may be prompted to run a configuration program.

Now let's see what's involved in capturing a single video frame. In the example below, we'll suppose you're using the Video Blaster card and associated software. For your video source, you can use a VCR (video cassette recorder), videodisc player, video camera, or other *NTSC* (National Television Standards Committee) or *PAL* (Phase Alternation Line) standard device.

? Which Cable?

You may need to do a little research to find the correct type of cable — with the appropriate connectors at each end — for linking your video source to the video capture card. Before purchasing a cable, decide whether you'll want to capture audio data along with video sequences (for example, from a VCR). If so, you'll need a cable that can carry audio as well as video signals.

1 Plug one end of an appropriate video cable into a video input jack on your video capture card. Connect the other end to the video source you're using.

2 In Windows Program Manager, double-click on the *Video Blaster* icon, and in the *Video Blaster* window, double-click on the *VBW Setup* icon.

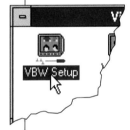

3 The *Video Blaster Setup* dialog box appears. Under *Video Standard*, choose the *NTSC* option (for North America and Japan) or *PAL* (for Europe). Under *Video Source*, choose the video input jack into which your video source is plugged (*Video 0* in this case).

4 Start up your video source. You should see the video appear on your monitor screen within a *VBW Setup View* window behind the *Video Blaster Setup* dialog box.

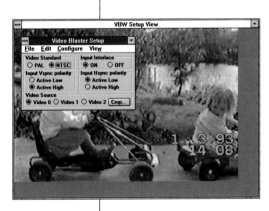

5 If you choose the *Align Video* command from the *Configure* menu, an *Adjust Video Alignment* dialog box appears. You can use the controls in this box to adjust the size and alignment of the video display to optimize the fit within the *VBW Setup View* window.

87

6 Close the *Video Blaster Setup* box by double-clicking on its control box. Save any changes. Now double-click on the *Video Kit* icon.

7 The video is now displayed in the *Video Kit* window. To capture a single frame, choose *Freeze* from the *Display* menu or press Ctrl-S at the appropriate moment.

8 A still image is displayed in the *Video Kit* window. To save this image as a file, choose *Save* from the *Display* menu. In the *Save Image* dialog box that appears, you can name and choose a file format (such as BMP, PCX, or TIFF) for the image. The resulting image file is no different from one created using a paint package or a scanner.

Moving Images

The overriding problem with capturing and displaying video sequences on a PC is the sheer amount of data involved — a few seconds of a full-screen video clip can involve 10 MB of data or more. This not only takes up a lot of disk space but also poses a problem of data transfer for the controlling hardware and software.

One solution is to limit the amount of data per video frame — for example, by restricting the video to a small window and by limiting the color depth in each image. Another approach is to compress the data in a captured sequence when you save it to disk. However, if it takes too long to decompress the data as you play the video, you'll get slow-moving, jerky results.

HARDWARE COMPRESSION AND DECOMPRESSION
Various systems and methods have been devised to tackle these problems. One method is to use special hardware that can carry out *compression* and decompression of video images very quickly. Unfortunately, the necessary hardware is very expensive. Furthermore, the compressed video cannot be displayed on another PC unless that PC has the correct decompression hardware.

Video Is Processor Intensive!
If you plan to do a lot of capturing, editing, and processing of video sequences, remember that video requires intensive use of your PC's microprocessor, memory, and disk space. For the best results, buy the biggest hard disk you can afford, as much RAM as possible, and the fastest PC available!

VIDEO FOR WINDOWS

One alternative to hardware compression and decompression is Microsoft's Video for Windows. This set of software utilities can be used (in conjunction with a video capture card) first to capture a video sequence and save it with associated sound to disk and then to edit the sequence and compress the data.

A major benefit of Video for Windows is that the compressed video sequences you create can be played in real time using Windows Media Player (see page 62) without any special hardware. This means that you can create a video clip for a multimedia show, put it on a floppy disk or portable hard disk (depending on the size of the clip), and then run it on almost any PC that has Windows.

Capturing a Real-Time Video Sequence

To illustrate exactly what's involved, let's look at how you can use Video for Windows to capture a short video sequence from a VCR and save it as an AVI file on your PC's hard disk (see "What Is AVI?" at left). First you need to install Video for Windows on your PC and also a Video for Windows device driver for your video capture card (device drivers for some video capture cards are supplied on a Drivers disk that comes with Video for Windows).

Next you connect your video source to your video capture card and your audio source either to the video capture card or to the sound card (see "Want Sound, Too?", above right). After verifying that you have at least 20 MB of free space on your hard disk, follow the procedure below.

What Is AVI?
Video for Windows stores the compressed video and audio data in a special file format called *AVI* (*audio/video interleaved*). AVI stores one frame of video, a matching amount of audio data, another frame of video, and so on, in adjacent portions of the storage medium. The AVI format greatly accelerates the possible rate of data retrieval, especially from relatively slow media such as CD-ROMs.

Want Sound, Too?
Many video capture cards, including the Video Blaster, cannot digitize audio signals. Therefore, if you want to combine audio data with a captured video sequence, you may need to connect your audio source to the Line In jack on your sound card. Video for Windows can take the captured frames from your video capture card and the accompanying digitized audio from your sound card and interleave the data in an AVI file.

1 First, open the VidCap utility by double-clicking on the *Video for Windows* icon in Windows Program Manager and then double-clicking on the *VidCap* icon.

2 The *VidCap* window opens. Choose *Set Capture File* from the *File* menu and, in the *Set Capture File* dialog box, name the capture file that will temporarily hold your video sequence. Then click on *OK*.

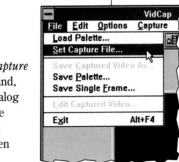

3 The *Set File Size* dialog box appears. Allocate at least 10 MB for your capture file. Then click on *OK*.

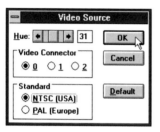

4 Next, choose *Video Source* from the *Options* menu and, in the *Video Source* dialog box, specify the video connector and the standard (*NTSC* or *PAL*) for the input video signal. Click on *OK*.

5 Now choose *Video Format* from the *Options* menu. In the *Video Format* dialog box, define your image dimensions and image format (color depth). An image size of 160-by-120 pixels and an 8-bit color depth will keep the amount of data per frame to a reasonable size. Click on *OK*.

6 Start your VCR. The moving images are displayed in the *VidCap* window. If you've chosen an 8-bit color depth for your video capture, you'll initially see black and white images — you'll need to define a palette of 256 colors to be used for the images. To do so, choose *Palette* from the *Capture* menu.

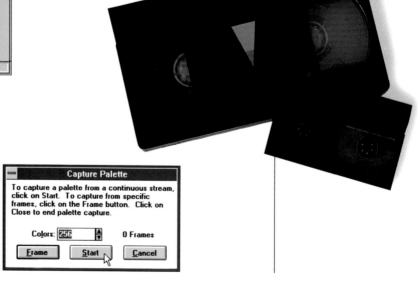

7 The *Capture Palette* dialog box appears. Start running the portion of the video that you eventually want to capture, click on *Start*, and a second or two later click on *Stop* and then on *Close*. VidCap samples colors from the video sequence and uses these to construct a palette of colors for use in the video display and for your eventual video capture.

8 Next choose *Audio Format* from the *Options* menu in order to define your audio options. In the *Audio Format* dialog box, set the sampling frequency, sample size, and number of audio channels, and then click on *OK*. A sample size of 8 bits, at a sampling frequency of 22 kHz, in mono, will provide reasonable audio quality. If you click on the *Level* button, you can access the *Set Record Level* dialog box. This allows you to determine whether the recording level of the audio input is set too high or too low.

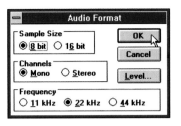

9 Now choose *Video* from the *Capture* menu.

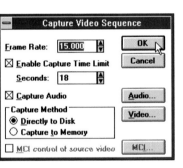

10 The *Capture Video Sequence* dialog box appears. Set the frame rate (15 frames per second will suffice as a start), check the *Enable Capture Time Limit* box, and set a limit of 20 seconds or less for the capture. Then rewind or fast forward your VCR until you reach a point about 15 seconds before the start of the video sequence you want to capture. Start up your VCR and click on *OK* in the *Capture Video Sequence* dialog box.

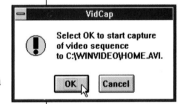

11 Another dialog box then appears. Click on *OK* when you want the capture to start.

12 When the video sequence has been captured, a warning box may appear stating how many frames were dropped during the capture. This indicates how well your system coped with the capture task that was set. If a high percentage of frames (more than 10 percent) was dropped, you may need to try again, setting a less demanding task in terms of image size and quality and/or the frame rate. Click on *OK* to close the warning box.

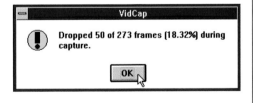

13 Now stop your VCR and choose *Save Captured Video As* from the *File* menu. In the *Save Captured Video As* dialog box, name your captured sequence, and then click on *OK*. The data is taken from your capture file and saved as a Microsoft AVI file under the new name. You can now close the *VidCap* window.

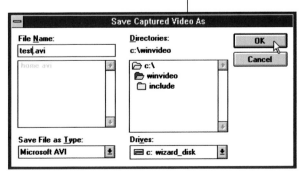

Editing a Video Sequence

Once you have recorded your video clip, you can view it and listen to the accompanying soundtrack using the VidEdit utility. VidEdit also allows you to edit the video and audio data. To open VidEdit, double-click on the *VidEdit* icon in the *Video for Windows* window. The *VidEdit* window opens. Choose the *Open* command from the *File* menu and then use the *Open Video File* dialog box to load the video sequence you have just captured and saved. If you choose *Statistics* from VidEdit's *Video* menu, the *Statistics* dialog box appears. This provides a summary of the size of the file, the number of video frames it contains, the frame rate, and the video and audio formats.

Edit Individual Frames?

Video sequences contain large numbers of bitmap images. One or more bitmaps in a sequence might require enhancement before the sequence is suitable for playback. Video for Windows includes a utility called BitEdit that you can use to edit individual frames. The *BitEdit* icon is placed in the *Multimedia Data Tools* group window when you perform a complete installation of Video for Windows.

VidEdit Features

VidEdit provides a variety of controls and tools for displaying particular frames in a sequence; selecting parts of a sequence; cutting, copying, or pasting sections of a sequence; and making various other modifications. In the example shown below, a section in the middle of a sequence has been selected for cutting.

Menu Bar

Toolbar
Provides buttons for operations such as saving, cutting, copying, pasting, and undoing.

Title Bar
Displays the filename of the active video clip.

Scroll Buttons
Used to move backward or forward through a sequence one frame at a time.

Mark In and Mark Out Buttons
Used to select a portion of a sequence for editing. To mark the beginning of the sequence to be edited, move the slider in the track bar until the appropriate frame is displayed, and then click on the Mark In *button. To mark the end of the sequence to be edited, move the slider again, and then click on the* Mark Out *button.*

Track Bar and Slider
Mark the position of the currently displayed frame within the sequence.

Playback Buttons
Used to play, stop, fast forward, or rewind a sequence.

Selected Portion of Sequence

Data-Track Buttons
Used to define whether your edits will affect the video or audio data in your AVI file, or both.

COMPRESSING A SEQUENCE

VidEdit also provides facilities for compressing a sequence. Compression reduces the amount of space the clip will occupy and improves playback by reducing the amount of data to be transferred from the storage medium per second (the data transfer rate).

Steps for Compression

1 Choose *Compression Options* from the *Video* menu. The *Compression Options* dialog box appears.

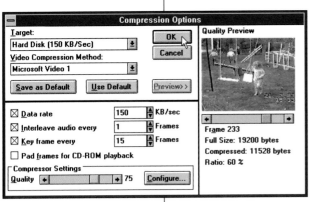

2 Click on the *Details* button and then the *Preview* button to display an enlarged dialog box, as shown at left. You can use this box to set a number of compression parameters and at the same time to get a preview of how the images in the compressed sequence will look. To compress a file for playback from a hard disk, try the settings shown at left. Later you can experiment with different settings.

3 After setting your compression options, click on *OK* in the *Compression Options* dialog box and then choose *Save As* from the *File* menu. The *Save Video File* dialog box appears.

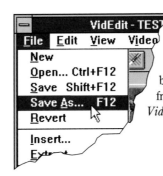

Balancing Speed, Size, and Quality

When creating video clips with Video for Windows, remember that there is always a trade-off between image size and quality and the smoothness of the display. If you want a large display window and high-quality images, the clip will take up huge amounts of disk space and will move slowly and jerkily. If you want to watch fast, real-time action, you will have to limit the size of the playback window and the image quality in terms of colors and resolution.

Compression Warning!

Compression involves some loss of data from the individual frames in a sequence, which inevitably means some reduction in image quality. Note also that even with compression, you may only be able to fit a very short video clip onto a floppy disk — around 9 seconds of video if you set a data transfer rate of 150 KB/sec and the floppy holds 1.44 MB of data.

4 Define a new name for the compressed file and click on *OK*. The video sequence will be compressed and saved under this name. The uncompressed file will remain with the original name. You can create several compressed files from the original uncompressed version, using different compression parameters, and view them using VidEdit or Media Player. Once you have a satisfactory compressed version, you can delete the uncompressed file.

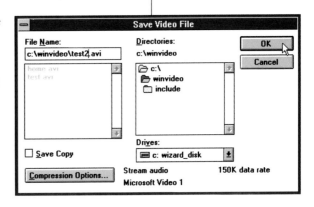

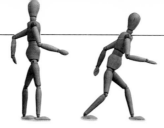

Get Animated

EVEN IF YOU DON'T HAVE VIDEO CAPTURE EQUIPMENT, you can still add eye-catching movement to your multimedia projects with animation software. Animation doesn't have to be complicated to work — adding movement to a logo, for instance, is easy to do and turns an everyday object into a dynamic display. Animation is also ideal for demonstrating how things work (for instance, to show the orbit of the planets around the sun).

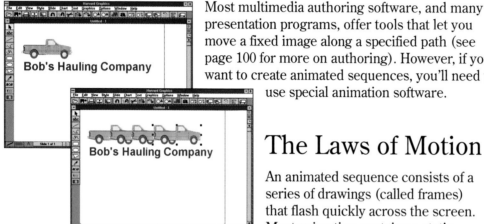

Most multimedia authoring software, and many presentation programs, offer tools that let you move a fixed image along a specified path (see page 100 for more on authoring). However, if you want to create animated sequences, you'll need to use special animation software.

Moving Objects
Presentation software such as Harvard Graphics (above) often offers tools for animating objects.

Making Tracks
By drawing the incremental positions in a dog's stride, you can create the impression of movement. This sequence was created with Animation Works Interactive.

The Laws of Motion

An animated sequence consists of a series of drawings (called frames) that flash quickly across the screen. Most animation contains a static background with an actor (often called a *cel* in animation programs) that appears to move across the scene. This illusion of movement is created by drawing the actor in a different position in each frame so that when the frames are run together at a high speed, the actor seems to move.

Like video, an animation sequence has to show a certain number of frames every second or the human eye will detect flickering. For smooth, professional looking cartoons, you'll need about 30 frames for every second of animation. Simpler animation, however, requires only about 10 frames per second.

Contour Lines
Tracing facilities let you view the previous frame of a sequence while you draw the next one.

SHADY CHARACTERS

Making each frame of a sequence slightly different from the last is not easy, although most animation software offers facilities to make this process easier. A common feature for simplifying the transition from one frame to the next is *tracing*.

Tracing makes the process easier by displaying a shadowy image of the previous frame under the current one you are creating. You can then trace over the previous image, changing only the parts that must change between frames.

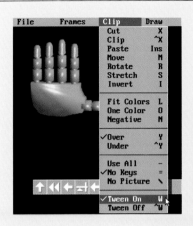

Between Moves

One particular function to look for in animation software is *tweening*. Tweening (derived from "between") means that you only need to draw certain frames of a sequence — the software works out the steps in between. This example, from PC Animate Plus, shows how it's done. The first stage (left) and last stage (bottom right) of the sequence were drawn; the software tweened the intermediate stages.

Creating Animation

Creating the Background

Animation sequences are usually produced in two main stages. The background and props normally stay the same throughout a sequence, so once they have been created they are simply copied into the required number of frames. When the actors have been created in all their incremental stages, they are also copied into the frames. To see how the process works, look at how a sequence is created in CorelMOVE!, an animation utility contained in CorelDRAW!

1 The Animation Screen is where the actual animation is pieced together and then displayed. The controls for playing a sequence are at the bottom of the window. On the left are buttons for creating each element of the sequence, such as the actors (third button down) and props (fourth button down).

2 To place a background (or prop) into the Animation Screen, click on the Prop button. The *New Prop* dialog box appears. You can either select a background from one you have on disk already (perhaps even a photograph you have scanned in) or create your own by clicking on the *Create New* option.

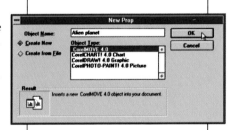

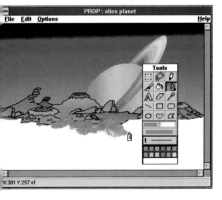

3 If you choose to create your own background, the Paint Edit window will open. Here you can see some of the tools available for creating images. In this case, the background will be for a sequence showing life on an alien planet.

4 Once the background has been created, choose *Apply Changes* from the *File* menu to place the background in the Animation Screen.

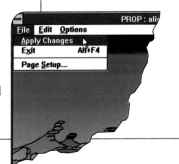

1 Draw the alien's first step. You might give him a pet on a string to hold.

CREATING AN ACTOR

Drawing your own actor is usually more complicated than creating a background because actors must give the impression of movement. In the case of the alien created here, for instance, the creature's legs must be drawn in several different positions to give the illusion that he is walking.

Like backgrounds, actors can also be imported into CorelMOVE! from other programs — for instance, a few frames of someone captured on video.

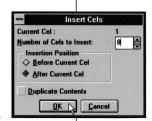

2 It will take about eight different leg positions to create the impression that the creature is walking, so add eight new cels to make a sequence. Because the alien and his pet will be in a different position in each cel, leave the *Duplicate Contents* option unchecked.

3 Set the Frame Counter on the bottom of the tool box to 2, and turn on the Onion Skin tracing option. A faint image of the first cel appears in the second cel, making it easy to draw the next stage in the alien's movement.

4 Once you've drawn eight cels (each slightly different from the last), the cels are placed in the Animation Screen with the background (the first cel goes into the first frame, the second cel into the second frame, and so on). Next, use the Path tool to specify the alien's path as it crosses the screen: the route is traced with the mouse.

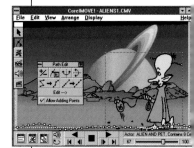

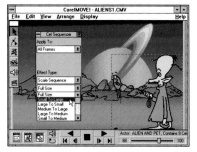

Size It Up
The Cel Sequencer *box lets you change the size of a cel over a selected number of frames so that actors seem to grow or shrink.*

ADDITIONS AND CHANGES

Most animation programs make it easy for users to change and edit the different elements of an animated sequence. You can usually select an element (an actor, for instance) and change its size or fade it in and out of a sequence. Most programs also allow you to add sounds (provided you have the right sound card and a microphone). Like backgrounds and actors, sounds can usually either be imported from other applications or created from within the animation program. The examples shown here are from CorelMOVE!

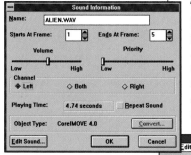

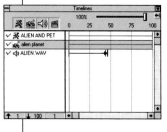

Timelines
The Timelines *box shows the frames that each object in an animation sequence appears in. You can edit the appearances by dragging the handle on the end of the timeline with the mouse.*

The Sound of Music
The Wave Editor *box (below) lets you record sound files, and you can use the* Sound Information *box (left) to stipulate exactly when the sound will play.*

Morphing

Morphing is the process whereby one image is metamorphosed into another. This example, from PhotoMorph, shows how it is done. You begin by loading the first image into the Start window and the second image into the End window. You then pair off points in each image; this point pairing tells the images where and how to merge. Once points have been specified, the program creates an animation sequence out of the process. When the sequence is played, the first image merges into the second.

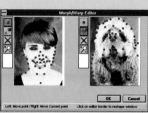

Simple Movements

Animation doesn't have to be complicated to be effective, nor does it have to include cartoon-type actors. An excellent use for animation is to explain how things work. In the example on the left, for instance, the background consists of a map of a battle area. The animation sequence is limited to information bubbles that pop up to explain troop movements, ships that "sail" up to the coast, and small explosions that occur as the two sides fire on each other. The retreat is illustrated with arrows that seem to move inland.

On the right you can see another example of how effective simple animation can be.

Pass It On

All animation programs contain an animation player, which lets you view a completed sequence on a PC that doesn't have animation software. When you buy an animation package, make sure that you can distribute this animation player along with the animation itself.

Like graphics files, animation sequences can be saved in a number of different formats. Sequences that are imported into documents or multimedia projects must be saved in a format that is recognized by the destination software. Common formats include FLI, FLC, and AVI (AVI is the same format used to save video clips captured using Video for Windows).

The Front Line
This animation sequence of the Battle of Bunker Hill from Microsoft Encarta) *shows how a simple line drawing can be animated.*

Moving Target
Nuclear fission is explained in this animation clip from Compton's Interactive Encyclopedia. *Here, no background was required; each frame is completely different, yet the animation was simple to create.*

5

CHAPTER FIVE

*A*ll Together Now

*In this chapter, we'll show you how
all the individual elements discussed so far
in this book come together when you create a multimedia product. Authoring software allows you to build
presentations by pulling together the individual elements
and defining how the software reacts to different responses
from the user. We'll look at some of the different types of
authoring packages and demonstrate how you might
plan and build a simple multimedia presentation using two different programs.*

AUTHORING SOFTWARE
PLANNING A MULTIMEDIA PRESENTATION
MICROSOFT VIEWER
AN ICON-AUTHORING PACKAGE

Authoring Software

B Y THIS TIME YOU KNOW HOW TO CREATE and manipulate all the different elements of multimedia — how to record and edit sound, develop an animation sequence, capture video clips, and create great pictures. Authoring software is used to assemble all these individual elements into a single, cohesive presentation or project.

Different Flavors of Software

Several different types of software programs are available for building multimedia presentations. At the simplest level are packages such as Microsoft PowerPoint and Macromedia Action!, which are designed to build slide shows. These are often referred to as presentation graphics programs rather than authoring software. Each of the slides in a show may include elements such as text, images, sounds, simple animation, and even video. However, the slides appear in a set order and in a linear sequence — these packages are not the solution if you want the user to be able to control the flow of the action.

AUTHORING PACKAGES
True authoring packages allow you to build interactivity into your product — you can put buttons or hotspots onto your screen that allow users to jump from one topic to another and choose which images they want to see, what sounds they want to hear, and so on. Different packages vary considerably in their sophistication and in the way you build a presentation.

Buttons for Playing, Stopping, and Rewinding a Scene

Timeline Window

Tools for Adding Motion, Special Effects, and Sound

Action!
With Action! (above), you build each slide or "scene" in a presentation with objects such as text, images, sounds, or video clips. You can use the program's Timeline window to arrange both the sequence in which the objects appear in each scene and the duration of their appearances.

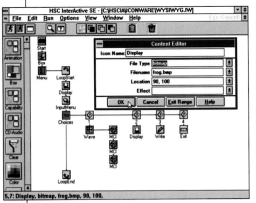

ICON-BASED PACKAGES
Icon-based authoring tools are among the easiest to learn to use. An example is HSC Interactive SE, which is based on a more expensive package, IconAuthor from AimTech.

HSC Interactive SE
With an icon-based package, you build your project based on actions — for example, the display of an image. The actions are represented by icons, which you link together on screen (left) to literally draw how your program works.

SCRIPT-BASED PACKAGES

Another group of authoring tools uses a special programming language to describe the multimedia application — you type in lines of commands or a "script," which is then executed by the authoring software. These packages give you excellent control over your project but can take a long time to learn. They are best suited to people who already have a good understanding of programming methods.

An example package of this type is ToolBook from Asymetrix Corporation. With ToolBook, you assemble a project or "book" from pages, which can contain text fields, buttons, and images. Authoring is based on "event handlers," which are script commands that define what happens when various events occur on a page, such as a click on a button. You build a project by writing the script (that is, all the commands for the presentation) and associating the handlers with objects such as buttons, hotspots, boxes, images, and so on.

MICROSOFT MULTIMEDIA VIEWER

Like ToolBook, Microsoft Multimedia Viewer is a script-based authoring tool in which you create your product by means of scripted commands that link the elements together and control the way text and graphics look on each page or "topic" in your project. However, Viewer provides features that allow you to write the authoring commands with little or no knowledge of a programming language. Viewer is a particularly useful package for putting together projects that contain a lot of text. Microsoft has created several multimedia titles, such as *Encarta* and *Cinemania*, using Viewer.

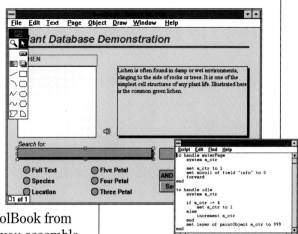

ToolBook
The screen above is taken from a gardening reference product in the process of being built using ToolBook. The smaller window contains a script that defines what happens when the user turns to a particular page in a ToolBook project.

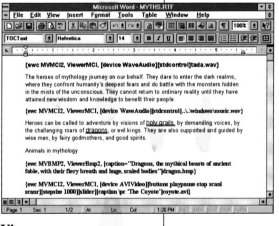

Viewer
When authoring with Viewer, you write and format all your text using Microsoft Word for Windows. You then insert authoring commands to add pictures, sounds, video clips, and animation and to control the flow of the presentation.

WHAT'S NEXT?

In the rest of this chapter, we'll be demonstrating how you might plan a very simple multimedia presentation and how you might then start building the presentation (or something similar) using either of two authoring packages — Microsoft Multimedia Viewer and HSC Interactive SE. If you don't own either of these authoring packages, it doesn't matter — you should still be able to follow the step-by-step sequences on pages 104 to 114 to see how these programs work.

What Else Do I Need?
Most authoring software comes with extra utilities to edit sound, pictures, and video. Although these utilities are often not as powerful or fully featured as stand-alone, dedicated editing packages, they are usually sufficient for all but the most ambitious projects. The more of these editing utilities an authoring system provides, the fewer specialized tools you will need.

Planning a Multimedia Presentation

OVER THE NEXT FEW PAGES, we'll show you how to plan a very simple multimedia presentation and build it using authoring software. You'll be developing a multimedia brochure about a great holiday destination in the sun — the island of Santo Dorado. You'll incorporate pictures of the island's beaches, tourist attractions, and leisure activities, and the sounds of local birds and of waves gently lapping on the shore — an irresistible advertisement for the resort!

The Santo Dorado Brochure

You've been invited by the government of Santo Dorado, a tiny island (and tax haven) in the Caribbean, to create a simple multimedia presentation about the island and its attractions. Visitors to Santo Dorado will be able to run the production on computer screens placed at key points such as the tourist office and the airport arrivals lounge.

You decide the presentation will consist of just three screens. User interaction will be limited to moving between the screens and accessing some sounds and video clips using a mouse.

Sketch It First!
Before authoring even the simplest multimedia project, you should work out what users will see and hear on each screen. You need to design the program's flow — how users will move between the screens and what buttons they can click on to start up items such as sound effects. You'll find it useful to do a sketch of each screen.

THE OPENING SCREEN
On the opening screen will be a welcoming image of the coast of Santo Dorado, with some palm trees, the deep blue sea, and a yacht sailing by. A headline will read **Welcome to Santo Dorado**. Below the image, there'll be buttons or text hotspots the user can click on to move to either of the other two screens — **Sights and Sounds** and **Sports and Leisure**. A Play button or text hotspot labeled **Click Here for a Special Message** will start up a voice-over extolling the virtues of Santo Dorado and explaining how to operate the brochure. The voice-over might incorporate some background sounds — perhaps a soothing soundtrack of waves lapping on the beach.

Headline

Main Image

Button or Text to Click on to Start Voice-Over

Buttons or Text to Click on to Access Screens 2 and 3

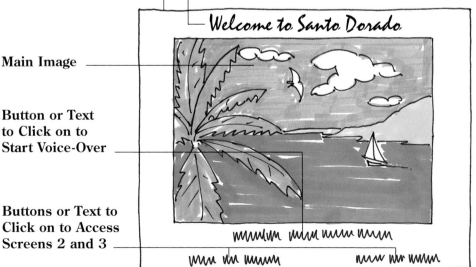

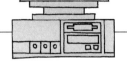

Welcome to Santo Dorado

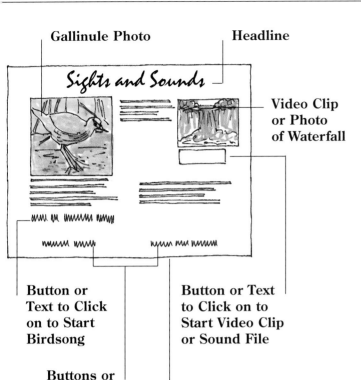

Gallinule Photo

Headline

Sights and Sounds

Video Clip or Photo of Waterfall

Button or Text to Click on to Start Birdsong

Button or Text to Click on to Start Video Clip or Sound File

Buttons or Text to Click on to Access Screens 1 and 3

THE SECOND SCREEN

As the user moves to the second screen, which is headlined **Sights and Sounds**, a short waveform or MIDI sound file will play — perhaps some calypso music. On the second screen, you'll want to show the viewers some of the unusual things they can see and hear on the island. Naturally, you'll want to include a picture of the Santo Dorado purple gallinule, a bird species unique to the island. The picture will have a caption and a hotspot the user can click on to hear the bird's unusual song. You'll also want to direct visitors to the island's spectacular "Roaring Thunder" waterfall. Users will be able to click on a Play button or text hotspot to see a video clip of the falls or hear a recording of the "roaring thunder." Again there'll be some short descriptive text.

In addition, hotspots on text labels or buttons at the bottom of the screen will provide the user with jumps back to the opening screen and to the third screen in the brochure.

THE THIRD SCREEN

The third screen, which is headlined **Sports and Leisure**, will have some items similar to those on the second screen — perhaps a video clip of a water-sport pursuit and a photograph taken inside one of the island's nightclubs, with some accompanying text and a sound button to start playing some reggae music. Again, buttons at the foot of the screen will provide access to the other two screens. We won't be explaining how you'd actually build this screen — the details would be very similar to those for the second screen.

Collecting Materials

Once you've planned your presentation, the next step is to make a list of the images, sound recordings, and other resources you'll need. Ideally, of course, your sponsors will provide an all-expenses-paid visit to Santo Dorado, where, armed with camera, tape recorder, and video camera, you would collect all the items you need! If the budget doesn't stretch to that, you may need to have the various resources sent to you or obtained from photograph, video, and sound libraries. You'll also need to record your voice-over for the opening screen and use a utility such as Sound Recorder to mix it with a background recording of waves lapping on the shore.

Perfect Your Materials!
After collecting the media clips for your presentation, the next step is to edit and perfect them using techniques touched on in previous chapters of this book. Name all your files so that the contents of each are easily identified from their names. Then save all the files within the same directory on your PC's hard disk.

Things to Get:

Images
Coast of Santo Dorado
Purple gallinule
Nightclub

Video Clips or Images
"Roaring Thunder" waterfall
Jet skier or scuba diver?

Sounds
Waves on beach
Gallinule song
Calypso music
Voice-over

Microsoft Viewer

VIEWER IS A SCRIPT-BASED authoring tool designed for non-programmers. You create a title by writing a script that controls the way text and graphics are displayed and links elements together. However, you don't need to know a programming language to write the script: Viewer lets you select the necessary instructions (known as authoring commands) from a list, using a utility called the Topic Editor. The Topic Editor works in conjunction with Microsoft Word for Windows: When you start Word from within Viewer, the Topic Editor is automatically made available.

How a Project Is Built

You begin the authoring process by typing all the text for the presentation into Word and then saving the file in a special format called RTF (rich text format). The RTF file and all the image and sound files for the presentation are then gathered together into a project file. The RTF file is opened again from within Viewer so that the Topic Editor becomes available. You can then add authoring commands to the RTF file; Word's formatting commands are also used to select fonts and position the text in the title.

Once the text has been formatted and the authoring commands added, the RTF file is run through the Viewer Compiler, which interprets the authoring commands and compiles the actual title.

Take a look at the steps below for a quick guide to the Viewer authoring process; the steps for building the Santo Dorado brochure begin on the opposite page.

The Viewer Tools
The Viewer Publishing Toolkit includes a number of authoring utilities. Project Editor is the main tool for developing titles: all the other tools can be launched from this utility.

Authoring Command for Hotspot

Authoring Command for Picture

The Viewer Authoring Process

Type all the text for the project into Word for Windows (or import it into Word from another application). Save the text file in RTF format and close Word.

Use Project Editor to create a project file.

Hotspot

Picture

From Project Editor, run the file through the Viewer Compiler to construct the title for viewing.

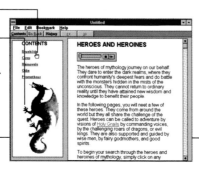

Open the text file from Project Editor and the Topic Editor becomes available. Use the Topic Editor to add authoring commands, and then close Word and return to Project Editor.

PREPARING TEXT FOR THE BROCHURE

To create the Santo Dorado brochure using Viewer, first enter the text in Word. All the text goes in one file, with text for different screens separated by page breaks (left). These separate screens are called topics.

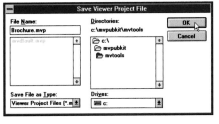

The brochure has three topics: the opening screen, Sights and Sounds, and Sports and Leisure. Each topic will link to the other two by means of hotspots. Word's table features are used to position the names of the hotspots (see how **Sights and Sounds** and **Sports and Leisure** have been positioned in the first topic, left). Then save the file in RTF format — this file has been named SANTOTXT.RTF.

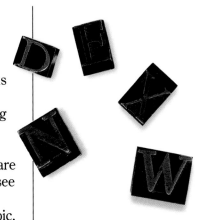

ORGANIZING FILES

Next you need to create a project file. The project file organizes and keeps track of all the different files that make up a title — text (RTF) files, video files, sound files, pictures, and so on.

Project files are created in Project Editor. Double-click on this icon in the Viewer group window, and the *Viewer Project Editor* window, shown at right, opens.

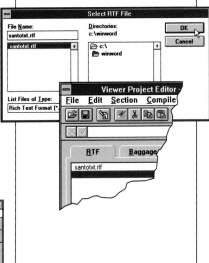

Edit Button

RTF Tab

Baggage Tab

Browse Button

Project File Window

Creating the Project File

1 Choose *Save As* from the *File* menu and give the title a name (for example, BROCHURE). Project files are always given an MVP extension; this will automatically be tagged onto the name.

2 To import your text file into the project file, click on the *RTF* tab and then click on the Browse button. In the *Select RTF File* dialog box (right), choose *SANTOTXT.RTF* from the WINWORD directory and click on *OK*. This file is then listed in the project file window (bottom right).

3 Adding sound, picture, and video files to the project file is similar to importing the text file, except that you select the *Baggage* tab before clicking on the Browse button. Using the *Select Baggage File* dialog box, choose the files you want and then click on *OK*. Once all the media files are in the Baggage section of the project file window, choose *Save* from the *File* menu.

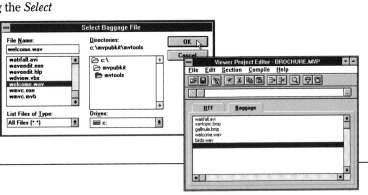

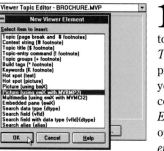

Adding Authoring Elements

Once you've added your text files and baggage files to the project file, you're ready to add the authoring commands. This is done in Word. First click on the *RTF* tab in the project file window and then click on the Edit button. SANTOTXT.RTF opens in Word. The *Viewer Topic Editor* icon appears at the bottom left-hand corner of the screen; whenever you want to add an authoring command to a text file, press a predefined hotkey to open the *Viewer Topic Editor* dialog box. (Consult the Viewer manual to see how to define the hotkey.)

Let's see how you would use authoring commands to display pictures.

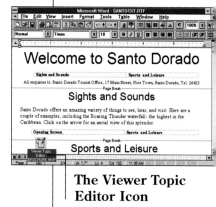

The Viewer Topic Editor Icon

How to Add Pictures to a Viewer Project

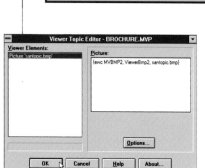

1 Place the insertion point where you want the image to go, and open the *Viewer Topic Editor* dialog box by pressing the hotkey. Because you are inserting a new command, the *New Viewer Element* window will also open. Choose *Picture [using ewX...]*, and click on *OK*.

2 The picture authoring command now appears in the *Viewer Topic Editor* dialog box, but no picture is specified. To name a picture, click on the *Options* button.

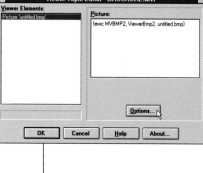

3 In the *Picture Filename* box in the *Picture Options* dialog box, type the name of the picture.

4 To add a caption to a picture, click on the *Caption* button in the *Picture Options* dialog box, and the *Picture Caption* dialog box will appear. Type the caption into the *Caption Text* box and click on *OK*.

5 When you click on *OK* in the *Picture Options* dialog box, the picture filename appears as part of the authoring command in the *Viewer Topic Editor* dialog box. Click on *OK*. Repeat steps 1 through 5 for each image in the brochure.

6 The picture authoring commands are now displayed in the text file (with captions, if the picture is captioned).

COMPILING THE BROCHURE

Once the authoring commands for pictures have been added to the text file, run the file through the Viewer Compiler to make sure that the brochure is taking the right shape. The Compiler interprets the authoring commands and constructs the brochure for viewing.

1 To use the Compiler, save the changes made to the text file and exit Word. In the *Viewer Project Editor* window, choose *Build* from the *Compile* menu.

2 The Viewer Compiler will run; you can watch while your brochure is compiled.

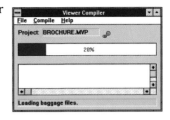

3 When the Compiler has finished, choose *Run Viewer On* from the *File* menu to view the brochure.

4 Watch as the brochure takes shape, with the text and pictures in place on each screen.

Once you have checked that the brochure is working, close the title. Back in Project Editor, open the SANTO-TXT.RTF file again by clicking on the Edit button. Now continue adding authoring commands.

CONTEXT STRINGS

Each topic in the brochure must now be given a label (known as a context string). Context strings identify the destinations for "jumps" between screens when users click on hotspots.

1 To label the opening screen, place the insertion point before **Welcome** in the first line of the topic and open the Topic Editor. In the *New Viewer Element* window, choose *Context string {# footnote}* and click on *OK*.

2 Type the name of the screen under *Context String* and click on *OK*.

3 A hash mark now appears before **Welcome** in the text. Word hides the actual context string, but you can view the label — and any other hidden commands in the text file — by choosing *View Footnotes* from the Word *Edit* menu.

CREATING A HOTSPOT

Now that each screen in the presentation has been given a context string, all the hotspots can be created. The Santo Dorado brochure has two hotspots in each topic — the two screen names that connect to the other topics in the brochure.

1 Highlight the name of the first hotspot text (**Sights and Sounds** on the opening screen) and open the *Viewer Topic Editor* dialog box.

2 Because text is selected, the *New Viewer Element* window will list only commands that relate to text. Choose *Hot spot [text]* and click on *OK*.

3 Back in the *Viewer Topic Editor* dialog box, select *Jump to* in the *Viewer Elements* box and type the context string of the hotspot destination (**Sights**) under *Context String*. Click on *OK*.

4 **Sights and Sounds** is now underlined, indicating that it is a hotspot.

5 After creating all the hotspots, save the text file and then compile the file again. By default, Viewer indicates a text hotspot by underlining and coloring the words; when you run the brochure, the cursor will change to a hand when it is positioned over a hotspot.

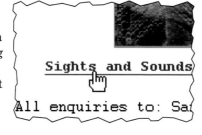

ADDING SOUND AND VIDEO

Viewer refers to sound, animation, and video as "multi-media sequences," and handles them in similar ways.

The following steps concentrate on showing how to add the welcoming voice-over to the opening screen of the brochure, but the same procedure could be used to add the video clip of the waterfall to the Sights and Sounds screen.

1 Position the insertion point and open the Topic Editor. In the *New Viewer Element* window, choose the *Multimedia....* command. Click on *OK*, and then click on the *Options* button in the *Viewer Topic Editor* dialog box.

2 In the *Multimedia Options* dialog box, drop down the options in the *MCI Device* box and choose *WaveAudio* (or *AVIVideo* to add a video clip). Type the name of the file you want under *Filename* and check the *Show Controller* box.

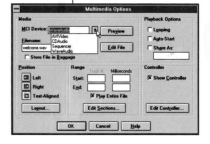

3 The standard multimedia controller in Viewer titles offers simple stop and play functions (right overlay). You can edit the appearance of this controller by clicking on *Edit Controller* in the *Multimedia Options* dialog box and choosing the desired options from the *MCI Controller* dialog box (right).

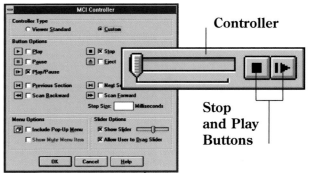

Controller

Stop and Play Buttons

4 Save the text file, and then run it through the Compiler for the final time. When the title is played by visitors to Santo Dorado, the first two screens will appear as shown here.

Righting the Wrongs!
If the Viewer Compiler encounters any errors during compilation, it records them in an error log. After compilation, the error log can be viewed; the location and cause of each error is specified, so mistakes can easily be rectified.

Other Viewer Tools

In addition to the actual authoring tools, Viewer includes a number of utilities for preparing the multimedia elements of a project.

The Hotspot Editor is used to create hotspots in a picture. After defining the location of a hotspot, you specify the type of action to be performed — for instance, jumping to a new topic, displaying a pop-up window, or playing a sound. Once again, context strings are used to specify hotspot destinations (see right).

BitEdit (see left) lets you perform simple editing of bitmapped images and is good for last-minute cropping and resizing. PalEdit is used to alter and add colors (including custom palettes) to an image.

WaveEdit can be used to record and edit waveform sound files. It offers a few more features than Windows Sound Recorder, although it is not as sophisticated as some of the wave file packages available commercially.

Finally, Convert will convert graphics and audio files into formats that are compatible with Viewer.

Enhancing Images
BitEdit can be used to edit bitmapped graphics.

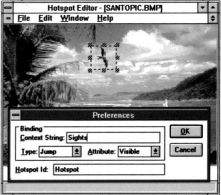

Picturesque Links
The Hotspot Editor lets you add hotspot regions to pictures.

An Icon-Authoring Package

REATING A MULTIMEDIA PRESENTATION by writing a program or script file takes a long time. It also takes time to understand and remember all the commands. An alternative method is to use an icon-based authoring system. Packages of this sort provide a visual programming environment that is easy to understand and put into action.

Building a Multimedia Program with Icons

The icon-authoring package we are going to use in this section is called HSC Interactive SE. With this program, you build a presentation by combining icons into a structure that depicts the flow of your project. The structure can include branched pathways to allow for choices made by the user. Each icon represents a particular action or task; for example, there are icons for displaying images on screen and playing sound files.

As you build the icon structure, you need to add "content" to some of the icons. This specifies more precisely the action that an icon should execute. For example, when you add content to a *Display* icon, you specify the filename of an image you want to display and where it should appear on the screen.

Building the Flow
With HSC Interactive SE, you build the basic flow-chart for your presentation by dragging icons from the toolbar on the left-hand side onto the main, blank part of the screen.

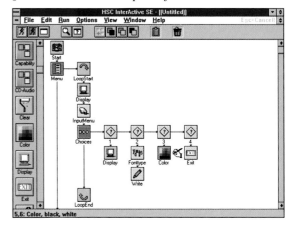

Pros and Cons
Once you've grasped a few basic rules that govern the order in which icons are executed, creating a simple presentation with a package like HSC Interactive SE is easy. However, if you want to build a project that contains a lot of text, Viewer would be a more suitable choice.

Icons at Your Fingertips

Here are some examples and descriptions of the icons available in HSC Interactive SE. Overall, 20 different icons are available, each with a distinct function.

 Write Icon
Displays a line of text.

 Display Icon
Displays an image on the screen.

 Wave Icon
Plays a waveform sound file.

 InputMenu Icon
Defines parts of the screen as selection areas or hotspots that, if clicked on by the user, cause program execution to flow along specified pathways in the icon structure.

 If Icon
Controls execution flow at pathway junctions.

 Color Icon
Defines the colors for items such as text and boxes.

Using HSC Interactive SE to Build Your Holiday Brochure

To give you a better idea of how an icon-authoring package works in practice, let's see how you would use HSC Interactive SE to build a second, slightly different, version of the Santo Dorado holiday brochure.

BUILDING THE OPENING SCREEN

The first task is to put the media files you want to use — like your sound and image files — into a directory structure that HSC Interactive SE automatically sets up on your hard disk when you install the program. Begin by putting your image files into a directory called C:\HSCIA\GRAPHICS and your sound files into a directory called C:\HSCIA\ AUDIO. After starting up HSC Interactive SE, proceed as follows:

Debug as You Build! As with any type of programming, you should run your application at frequent intervals as you build it, make a note of any "bugs" or imperfections in the program, fix these, and then proceed.

1 Choose *New* from the *File* menu, and in the *File Save As* dialog box, name the program file you are going to create (the extension IW is added automatically). This file will store the icon structure that you'll build and the content of each icon.

2 Because the first screen in your presentation will contain a number of options from which the user can select, the first icon you'll need is a *Menu* icon. Drag this into place below the *Start* icon. The *Menu* icon is a "composite" icon. It actually consists of a cluster of icons (right) that make it easier to display an image on the screen, define selection areas (hotspots), and specify what happens when different options are chosen.

3 Next, insert a *Clear* icon immediately below the *LoopStart* icon in the *Menu* icon composite. The *Clear* icon clears the screen to a single-color background — you can use this icon to set up a white background for your opening screen. After placing the *Clear* icon, double-click on it.

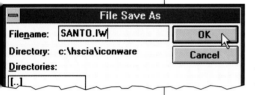

4 The *Content Editor* dialog box opens. Because the default background is white, just click on *OK*.

5 Now double-click on the *Display* icon immediately below the *Clear* icon.

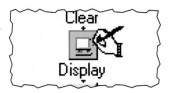

6 In the *Filename* box in the *Content Editor* dialog box, specify the image file for your opening screen (SANTOPIC.BMP). In the *Location* box, enter the X and Y coordinates (in pixels) at which you would like the top left corner of the image placed on the screen. Then click on *OK*.

Keep It Simple!
Even with a relatively intuitive authoring tool such as HSC Interactive SE, you should keep your initial attempts at building a presentation very simple and straightforward. If you get too ambitious, you may quickly end up with a vast structure of icons, and the flow of the application can become difficult to understand, modify, or debug!

7 At this point, you can click on the Run Application button at the top left of the screen to see how the program you have written so far behaves. The screen should clear to a white background and your main image should appear. Press Esc to go back to your icon structure.

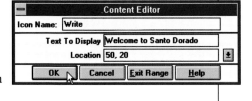

8 For each line of text on your opening screen, you need to add a *Write* icon to your structure. Before the first *Write* icon, place *Fonttype* and *Fontsize* icons. Using the content editors for these two icons, specify the font and font size for the headline text.

9 After double-clicking on the *Write* icon, write the headline text and indicate its location on your opening screen. Add other *Write* icons to specify other text items and their locations. Specifically, you want the words **Click Here for a Special Message** to appear beneath your main image and the words **Sights and Sounds** and **Sports and Leisure** to appear at the foot of the screen. Remember that with any change of font size, the relevant *Write* icon must be preceded by a *Fontsize* icon and the new font size specified.

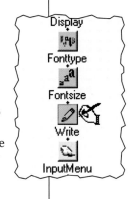

10 With a little trial and error and some adjustments to the positioning of your text and images, the finished opening screen might look something like that shown at right.

DEFINING THE HOTSPOTS

The next step is to define the hotspots on your opening screen and specify what happens when you click on these screen areas. For example, you want your voice-over to start playing when the user clicks on the words **Click Here for a Special Message**, and you want the second screen to open when the user clicks on the words **Sights and Sounds**.

To build these choices into your program, you use the *InputMenu* icon and the *If* icons (labeled 1, 2, 3, and 4) that are already built into your icon structure. Using the *InputMenu* icon, you define, in a specific order, the selection areas (hotspots) on your opening screen. By default, if the user clicks on the first selection area you define, the execution of the program flows to the first icon placed below *If* icon number 1. If the user clicks on the second selection area, the program flows to the first icon placed below *If* icon number 2, and so on.

Click Here for a Special Message

Sights and Sounds   Sports and Leisure

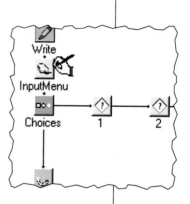

1 Double-click on the *InputMenu* icon below your last *Write* icon.

2 Next to *Selection Areas* in the *Content Editor* dialog box, define rectangular areas for your hotspots. Define each area with a group of four numbers (the first two numbers specify X and Y coordinates, in pixels, for the top left corner of the selection area; the third and fourth numbers specify the width and depth of the area). The first selection area should cover the words **Click Here for a Special Message** on your opening screen. The second should cover the words **Sights and Sounds**.

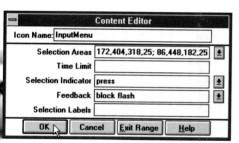

3 When you run your application again, you will see that a rectangular block or box appears when you point to each selection area with the mouse.

4 Now start building icon structures below the numbered *If* icons. Below *If* icon number 1, drag a *Wave* icon. You'll use this icon to specify that the voice-over sound file should play. The *Wave* icon is a composite icon that incorporates three *MCI* (media control interface) icons. These icons automatically execute MCI commands for opening, playing, and stopping waveform sound files.

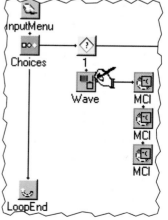

?

Want Video?
HSC Interactive SE can be used to display live video clips (from a live video source) as part of a presentation. However, there is no facility to display a video clip stored as an AVI file on your hard disk.

5 After double-clicking on the *Wave* icon, use the *Content Editor* dialog box to specify the waveform sound file to be played (WELCOME.WAV).

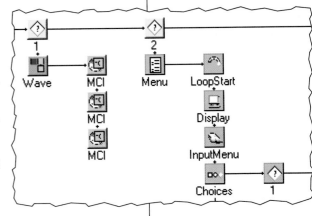

6 Next, start building an icon structure below *If* icon number 2. This part of your structure will open up your second screen, **Sights and Sounds**. Again, this screen will contain some selection areas, so it should start with a *Menu* icon.

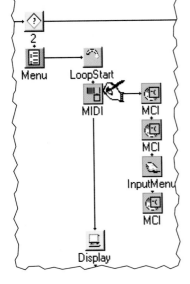

7 As your second screen opens, you want some MIDI music to play, so place a *MIDI* icon below the *LoopStart* icon. Using the *Content Editor* dialog box, specify the filename of the MIDI file you want to use. Like the *Wave* icon, the *MIDI* icon is a composite. The *InputMenu* icon in the MIDI composite specifies, by default, that when the user clicks anywhere on the screen the MIDI file stops playing and the execution flow continues.

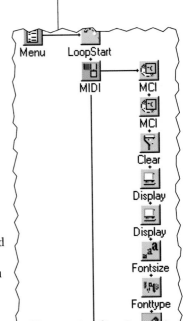

8 Within the MIDI icon composite, add a series of *Display*, *Font*, and *Write* icons to build all the text and images you want for the second screen. Similarly, using an *InputMenu* icon, define your selection areas on the second screen.

9 With a little trial and error, you could build a second screen that looks something like the one shown at left. Your next step would be to define the sound files or video clips that play when you click on selection areas such as the words **Click for Gallinule Song**.

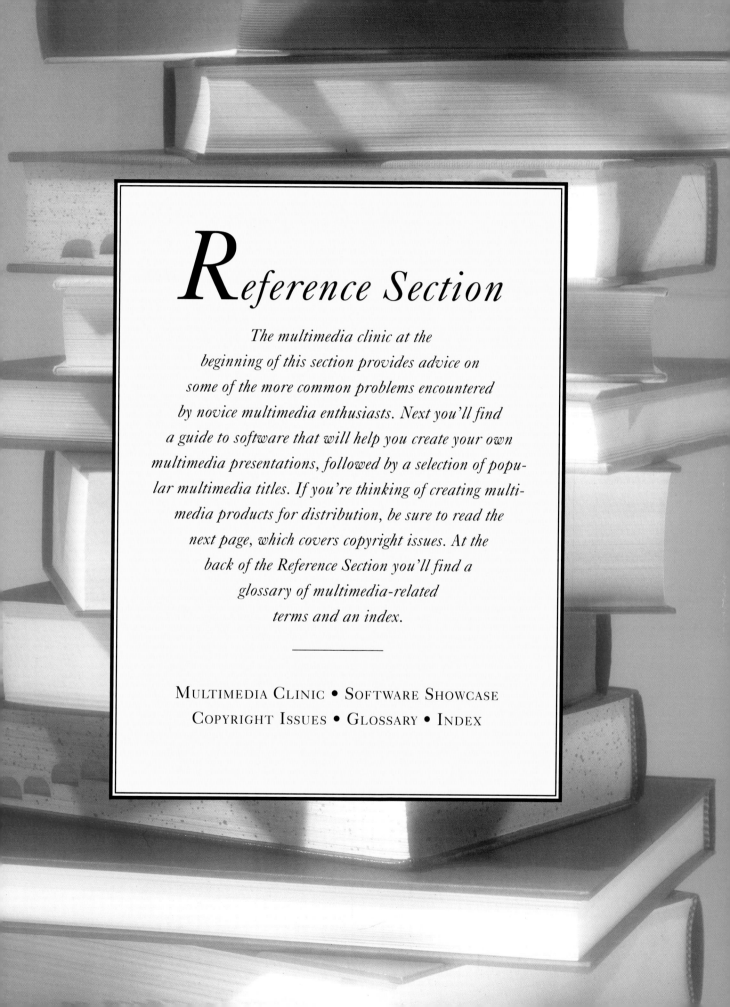

Reference Section

The multimedia clinic at the beginning of this section provides advice on some of the more common problems encountered by novice multimedia enthusiasts. Next you'll find a guide to software that will help you create your own multimedia presentations, followed by a selection of popular multimedia titles. If you're thinking of creating multimedia products for distribution, be sure to read the next page, which covers copyright issues. At the back of the Reference Section you'll find a glossary of multimedia-related terms and an index.

MULTIMEDIA CLINIC • SOFTWARE SHOWCASE
COPYRIGHT ISSUES • GLOSSARY • INDEX

Multimedia Clinic

HIS SECTION PROVIDES ANSWERS to some common questions relating to multimedia computing. If you are dissatisfied with the speed of your PC, check out the box on the opposite page for some tips on optimizing performance.

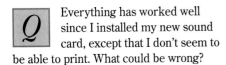

Q Why does nothing happen when I try to record or play sounds using the Windows Sound Recorder utility?

A Some sound cards need to have their record and playback volumes set using mixer software. Check your sound card's manual for the name of the mixer program, and then run this utility. You may find that the speaker or microphone volume has been set to zero.

Q Everything has worked well since I installed my new sound card, except that I don't seem to be able to print. What could be wrong?

A Like the sound card, the printer port uses a particular IRQ (interrupt request) setting. If the sound card and the printer port are both set to the same IRQ value, your PC won't know whether to send data for printing to the sound card or to the printer port! Choose another IRQ setting for the sound card — and change the configuration for the sound card's device driver — so that both the sound card and the printer can work properly.

Q At the back of my sound card are two jacks but no labels. I'm not sure which is the microphone input. How can I check?

A It's important not to plug the microphone into the speaker jack, since you could easily damage your microphone. The safest way to check which jack is which is to plug the speakers into one socket and try playing a sound. If you can hear the sound, you've got the right socket for the speakers; if you don't hear anything, switch the speakers to the second socket. That way you won't risk damaging your microphone.

Q When I use my sound card to play waveform files, everything sounds great. Why can't I hear anything when I try to play MIDI files?

A First, check that your sound card has a built-in synthesizer. Some older cards can transmit MIDI signals but cannot generate sounds. If your card has a built-in synthesizer, you have probably incorrectly configured the device driver for the synthesizer. Refer to your sound card's manual for instructions on running a test and configuration program.

Playing Videos

Q When I play video clips from CD-ROM discs, why is the action so jerky?

A Older CD-ROM drives have slow access speeds and/or data transfer rates, and this causes video action to look jerky. Video will also not perform well on a microprocessor that is slower than an 80386 (for instance, an 80286). Your only solution in these cases is to upgrade the microprocessor and/or purchase a faster CD-ROM drive.

Q When I record video clips using my video capture card I can hear the sound. Why don't I hear any sound when I play the clip back?

A Many video capture cards cannot actually record sound — they simply pass audio signals straight to the speaker port — and this is probably your problem. The solution is to connect your audio source to the Line In jack on your sound card. For example, you'll probably find that a cable supplied for connecting a video cassette recorder to a video capture card contains two wires marked "audio." These normally end in phono connectors, so you'll need to plug these into a phono-to-jack converter and then plug the jack connector into the sound card.

CD-ROM

Q I understand that since my CD-ROM drive is controlled by a SCSI card, it's possible to use the card to control other SCSI devices, such as scanners. So why is it that when I plug a scanner into the CD-ROM controller card, nothing works?

A Many CD-ROM upgrade kits use a proprietary controller. This is similar to a SCSI controller except that you can't connect other SCSI devices to it. Check the specifications in your CD-ROM drive manual. If you find that the controller does allow other devices to be connected, the problem may be that your CD-ROM drive has a terminator plug on it. This must be removed when another device is connected to the CD-ROM drive or controller card. Lastly, each SCSI device needs to have its own address. You'll find a little bank of switches on the back of each device that can set the SCSI address. Make sure that the addresses for the scanner and the CD-ROM drive are different.

Q Sometimes when I switch on my PC, the CD-ROM driver loads, yet when I try to access the CD-ROM drive, I get an error message telling me that no drive is present.

A The most common cause of this error message is that the software required to control the CD-ROM drive was not installed properly. Re-install this software and restart your computer. Also, if you have an external CD-ROM drive, try turning it on before you turn on your PC.

Display

Q Sometimes when I import images into an application, they are displayed in strange colors. What could be wrong?

A Every software application has a palette to which it refers when displaying color on screen. When an image is transferred from one application to another, the new application often has to guess which colors it should use to display the image, and sometimes it comes up with the wrong colors. One way to avoid this is to save your image files in TIFF format, which usually encodes the correct palette into the image file. PCX files do not contain palette information.

Q I tried to select a new display mode for my monitor, but when I tried to restart Windows, the screen went blank. What's the problem?

A Your monitor probably doesn't support the display mode you selected. You'll need to go back to the setup screen. Leave Windows by pressing Alt-F4, waiting a few seconds, and then pressing Enter. When you are back at the MS-DOS prompt, go into the WINDOWS directory by typing **CD \WINDOWS** and pressing Enter. Type **SETUP**, press Enter, and change the display mode to its former settings.

Q I have set my display at a higher resolution than I usually use, which shows crisp graphics but which seems to have slowed the speed at which the images are displayed. Can I do anything about this?

A If you increase the resolution, you also increase the amount of data that your PC has to move to display images. You must have a pretty good eye to spot this, since it's still fast. Performance degrades most noticeably when you increase both the resolution and the number of colors. To speed up image display, try decreasing the resolution or the number of colors or both.

Tuning Your PC for Optimal Performance

Multimedia applications are partial to high-powered PCs. They'll gobble up all the resources you can give them and still seem slow! The tricks described below will help you get the most out of your multimedia PC.

■ You can optimize your PC's memory usage with the MemMaker utility provided with MS-DOS 6. To run this utility, type **MEMMAKER** at the MS-DOS command prompt. Press Enter and then choose the *Express Setup* option. You will be asked if you use expanded memory; if you use only Windows programs, choose no.

■ Make the most of the Windows swap file. A swap file (also known as virtual memory) is an area on your hard disk used by Windows to temporarily save data when it runs out of RAM. There are two types of swap files — permanent and temporary. Windows runs faster with a permanent swap file. Sometimes Windows sets or recommends a swap file that is larger than necessary, and this slows down your PC.

To view your current swap file settings, double-click on the *386 Enhanced* icon in Windows Control Panel. In the *386 Enhanced* dialog box, click on the *Virtual Memory* button. The current swap file size and type will be displayed. If your swap file is temporary, refer to your Windows manual to find out how to create a permanent swap file. If you already have a permanent swap file, try to reduce the file size by 100 KB at a time to see if there's any improvement in your PC's speed.

■ Defragment your hard disk every few weeks. Using the Defrag utility available with MS-DOS 6, you can optimize the way data is stored on your hard disk, which should result in faster disk access times. To access Defrag, type **DEFRAG** at the MS-DOS command prompt.

Q What setup should I use with scanning software when I am scanning images to display on my monitor? And what about scanning an image I later want to print?

A Most scanners work at an average resolution of 300 dpi (dots per inch). However, monitors display images at a resolution of between 60 and 75 dpi, so it's unnecessary to use a scanning resolution higher than 100 dpi. Remember, though, that monitors can display thousands of colors or gray shades, so you should scan images with the maximum number of colors or gray shades. Printers work in the opposite way, so if you are scanning an image to print, use the highest resolution but don't worry too much about the number of gray shades.

Upgrading

Q I want to spend a little money on upgrading my multimedia PC. What's the most cost-effective purchase to make?

A Buying more RAM (random access memory) is the cheapest way to upgrade your PC and will also give you the best performance boost for your money. If your processor allows it, you can also install an OverDrive chip (which doubles the clock speed), but this doesn't offer as big a jump in performance as an increase in RAM.

Software Showcase

THIS GUIDE TO SOUND, IMAGE, AND AUTHORING PACKAGES supplements the software information you have already encountered in the book. The title of each package is followed by the publisher's name (in parentheses). On page 120, we take a look at some popular multimedia titles. Note that this is not intended to be a definitive guide; new packages come out all the time, so ask your dealer what's available.

Sound

The software for creating and editing sound falls into two categories: waveform programs and MIDI sequencers. Waveform editors handle digital audio and are used for voice recordings; MIDI programs are used to record, edit, and play MIDI files.

TRAX FOR WINDOWS (PASSPORT DESIGNS)

This MIDI sequencer for PCs will record up to 64 tracks. Composing, editing, and arranging music is easy with the graphic interface, and the tape-recorder format makes Trax a good package for novices.

MUSIC MENTOR WITH RECORDING SESSION (MIDISOFT CORPORATION)

This title includes Music Mentor, a guide to music reading skills and composition, and Recording Session, a MIDI sequencer.

SEQMAX PRESTO! (BIG NOISE SOFTWARE)

This sequencer offers four different methods of viewing notes — piano-roll, drum-grid, event list, and score page. Four hundred drum patterns are included. This is a good package for those new to sequencing.

WAVE FOR WINDOWS (TURTLE BEACH SYSTEMS)

This fun, easy-to-use waveform recording program provides a highly visual interface. It works with 8- or 16-bit files, offers 11-, 22-, or 44-kHz sampling rates, and helps you add a range of professional effects to sound files.

SOUND IMPRESSION (ASYSTEM)

This 16-bit recording and editing waveform program lets you mix up to 16 tracks of digital audio into a single composition. It's sophisticated, yet easy to use.

MCS STEREO (ANIMOTION)

This advanced waveform recording and editing program also includes a MIDI sequencer. The graphical interface is designed to look like a modern stereo unit, and the program has an extensive interactive tutorial.

Graphics

There are three main types of graphics software: drawing programs (for vector drawings), paint programs (for creating bitmap pictures), and image editing programs.

Vector-based drawing packages are good for drawing very precise lines, curves, and shapes. Bitmap drawing packages are not as precise as vector programs, but they are usually easier to use. Image editing programs are used to edit existing bitmap images, although they usually also offer bitmap drawing tools.

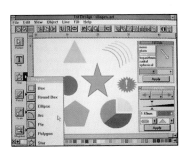

ARTS AND LETTERS APPRENTICE (COMPUTER SUPPORT CORPORATION)

This easy-to-use package is designed especially for beginners and provides a good introduction to the types of drawing tools found in vector programs.

1ST DESIGN (GST SOFTWARE PRODUCTS)

This package is aimed at users who are new to graphics software. It offers both vector and bitmap tools, and the amount of on-screen help makes it an easy package to learn.

INTELLIDRAW (ALDUS CORPORATION)

Aimed at the novice illustrator, this unusual vector drawing program includes a library of predrawn shapes from which users can create their own designs.

ADOBE ILLUSTRATOR (ADOBE SYSTEMS)

This vector-based drawing program is especially strong on text handling. You can even design a new typeface with the program! The package includes a large selection of predrawn artwork (textures, patterns, symbols, etc.). It has a steep learning curve, so it is not suitable for beginners.

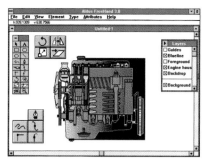

ALDUS FREEHAND (ALDUS CORPORATION)

This vector program offers a useful 99 levels of undo and an unusually large tool palette. Although not really for novices, it is fairly easy to use.

FRACTAL DESIGN PAINTER (FRACTAL DESIGN CORPORATION)

This fun, easy-to-use program offers a huge range of tools for simulating natural tools and textures — chalk, watercolor, canvas, different paper textures, and so on. You can even produce pictures in the style of Van Gogh or Seurat, or import an image and use it as a guide for painting your own.

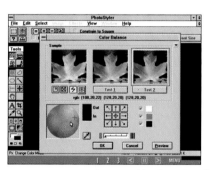

PHOTOSTYLER (ALDUS CORPORATION)

PhotoStyler is primarily an image editing program and comes with scanning software. You can also create original images with the program, and its ease of use and its functionality make it a useful purchase. However, it is pricey and is really meant for the serious illustrator.

HSC DIGITAL MORPH (HSC SOFTWARE)

This morphing program uses lines rather than points to merge images. Special "warp" facilities allow you to create caricatures or similarly distort images. Image retouching tools are also provided.

Clip Media and Shareware Programs

Clip media CD-ROM software packages offer ready-made images, sounds, and video clips that you can use in your presentations. Although usage is generally royalty free, you do occasionally have to pay usage fees, so read the accompanying copyright notice very carefully.

Many software vendors sell collections of sounds and pictures culled from shareware and public domain software at a very low price. Of course, if you have a modem and subscribe to an on-line service, you can simply download your own clips.

CORELDRAW! (COREL SYSTEMS CORPORATION)

In addition to the main vector drawing package, CorelDRAW! offers a number of other utilities. CorelPHOTO-PAINT!, for instance, can be used to create bitmap pictures or edit existing images, and Corel-SHOW! lets you create a slide show out of screen images. An animation program, an image-filing system, and facilities for creating charts are also included. This wealth of utilities makes CorelDRAW! a desirable purchase, although it is not really for novices.

Authoring

Assembling your own pictures, video clips, sound files, and text into an interactive presentation is fun, satisfying, and easier to do than you might think.

SUPER SHOW & TELL (ASK ME MULTIMEDIA CENTER)

This is a graphic, easy-to-learn program for creating interactive presentations. The presentation is built up around the concept of a slide show. You position media objects (including text) on each slide, then connect slides by designating these media elements as hotspots that jump to other slides or initiate actions. Presentations can be set to run automatically.

TEMPRA SHOW (MATHEMATICA)

Tempra Show lets you create presentations by building up lines in a script. Each line specifies an event (an event can be text, audio, images, or video), and the lines are linked together to create a presentation. Although easy to use, the program takes time to learn.

AUTHORWARE PROFESSIONAL (MACROMEDIA)

This package uses drag-and-drop icons to represent text, sound, and image elements and to create the flow of a presentation. It allows an unusually high degree of user interaction with the finished product. Newcomers to authoring might find the program difficult to learn, although it offers a very visual approach to building presentations.

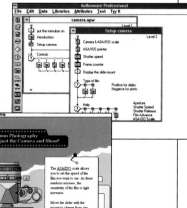

Information and Entertainment

There are thousands of multimedia titles on the shelves, covering many subjects. Here is a further glimpse of some of the available titles.

LEARN TO SPEAK SERIES (HYPERGLOT SOFTWARE)

Learn another language with these self-study language tutors. The emphasis is on learning words within a real-life context, rather than as strings of vocabulary. You can also record your own pronunciation and then compare it to a recording by a native speaker.

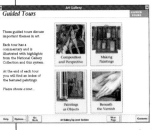

MICROSOFT ART GALLERY (MICROSOFT CORPORATION)

Take a tour of London's National Gallery, with 2,000 paintings dating from 1300 to this century. Animation is used to explain the techniques of the great artists, and the history and social conditions of the artist's time put paintings into their proper context.

BATTLE CHESS (INTERPLAY)

A new experience in the game of chess, this title contains animated pieces that play out battles when a piece is taken. A detailed animated tutorial will teach beginners to play chess.

SPACE ADVENTURE (KNOWLEDGE ADVENTURE)

Take a highly interactive voyage into space, with plenty of video, sounds, and images. You can read about space missions, ponder how the universe was formed and what it is made of, and follow the search for extraterrestrial life.

TIME ALMANAC (COMPACT PUBLISHING)

This title is produced annually and consists of the previous year's articles and images from *Time* magazine, as well as a collection of features from previous decades. Video clips are included, and you can test your knowledge of current affairs with the NewsQuest quiz.

THE WAY THINGS WORK (DORLING KINDERSLEY/ HOUGHTON MIFFLIN)

Based on David Macaulay's best selling book, this title uses hundreds of animation clips to explain the workings of everything from aircraft to X-rays.

THE BIG GREEN DISK (MEDIA DESIGN INTERACTIVE)

Designed to give users an overview of ecological problems, this title explains the origins of the difficulties facing the earth, details possible solutions, and includes interviews with leading experts.

RETURN TO ZORK (ACTIVISION)

This challenging adventure game features excellent graphics, real actors, and full-motion video footage. The title is the fifth in a series.

WORLD VISTA (APPLIED OPTICAL MEDIA)

More than a simple atlas, this title includes images and sounds from over 200 countries. In addition to history and politics, topics covered include agriculture, health, education, and crime. Users can also learn common phrases in 25 languages.

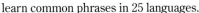

INTRODUCTION TO CLASSICAL MUSIC (ATTICA CYBERNETICS)

Aimed at the novice listener, this title details the various types of classical music and explains music terminology. Seven different search methods are available to guide users through the four hours of music clips.

MACMILLAN DICTIONARY FOR CHILDREN (MAXWELL ELECTRONIC PUBLISHING)

This product offers an entertaining way for children to learn; every word has an audio pronunciation, and some entries include animated sequences.

Copyright Issues

O NE OF THE BIGGEST PROBLEMS facing anyone creating a multimedia presentation is that of copyright. You might feel that the addition of a few bars of a well known song will turn your project into a masterpiece, or that a text explanation simply won't work unless it's illustrated with an image you've seen in a book. You have a scanner, you have the musical recording you want to use, and you have the necessary equipment. What you don't have, however, is permission.

Artistic Protection

Copying an image, a piece of music, or written material (text) without permission is a breach of copyright law. The exact terms of copyright law vary from country to country, but all industrialized countries protect artistic, written, musical, and other intellectual property from being copied. Copyright law gives the copyright owner exclusive rights to reproduce a work, distribute copies of it, modify the original in any way, and display the work in public.

The following information is a guide to copyright law in developed countries. For information relating to a specific country, contact the Copyright Office in that country.

LIFE AFTER DEATH
In most countries, a work is automatically protected by copyright law from its date of creation, although a few countries require the work to be registered for copyright protection.

Copyrights do not last forever, but don't assume that the protection expires when the copyright owner dies. A copyright lasts for a specified time after the death of the copyright owner. When the artist and the copyright owner are not the same person (for instance, magazine publishers usually own the copyright for work used in their publications), the copyright expires a specified time after the work is published.

When the period ends, the work falls into the public domain and anyone is free to copy it without permission.

THE FAIR USE CLAUSE
In most countries, there is an area of the law — the fair use privilege — that allows copying without permission in certain circumstances. Copying for the purpose of criticism or commentary — for instance to illustrate a news report — is allowed under the fair use clause.

This clause also makes it difficult for the copyright owner to prosecute when only a small part of the original work has been copied. If the amount and importance of the piece used is insignificant compared with the original, a court would probably rule it to be fair use. However, fair use can be a gray area of the law and should not be interpreted too liberally. Under most copyright laws, only the copyright owner is allowed to copy his or her work and adapt or modify it.

In short, do not copy, adapt, or modify any original work, or even part of that work, without obtaining permission first. If you intend to distribute or sell something that contains an original work (or part of an original work), make sure that you get the permission in writing.

TRADEMARKS
Copyright extends to all artistic, written, and intellectual property. It doesn't cover logos, trade names, slogans, or jingles, although if these are registered as trademarks, you are not allowed to copy or use them without the permission of the trademark owner.

COPYING FROM CD-ROM TITLES
Many CD-ROM titles allow you to copy text, pictures, and audio for your personal use. Topics can be printed for research purposes, for instance, or images can be copied for use as Windows wallpaper. Note that permission to copy varies from title to title; always read the section on your copyright responsibilities before copying anything from a title.

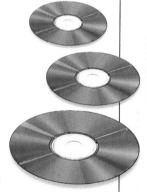

How to Get Copyright Permission

When seeking permission to copy a published work, it is best to contact the publisher of the work first — for example, the publisher of a magazine that contains an image or piece of text you want to use. In the case of recorded music, contact the record company. The publisher or record company may be able to grant permission outright to copy material or will be able to advise you further if permission is required from the original creator of the work.

If it's not clear who owns the rights to a work, you can contact the Copyright Office in the country of origin. Most of these offices will perform copyright-registration searches for a fee. Some countries also have agencies that perform searches, although such searches are usually quite costly.

GLOSSARY

This glossary contains definitions for a number of technical terms used in this book and also for a selection of other multimedia terms. Terms in *italics* refer to other glossary entries.

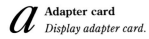

Adapter card
Display adapter card.

ADC
Analog to digital conversion.

Amplitude
The strength of a sound signal at a given moment.

Analog signal
A continuously varying voltage or wave pattern, such as a sound wave.

Analog to digital conversion
The conversion of an *analog signal* into *digital data*, such as that carried out by a *sound card* when digitizing a sound wave as a *waveform file*.

Animation
The display of a sequence of drawings that gives the illusion of lifelike movement.

Audio/video interleaved
A *file format* used for storing video clips. In AVI format, the data for successive video frames is interleaved with accompanying audio data.

Authoring software
Programs used to create *interactive multimedia*.

AVI
Audio/video interleaved.

Bit
An electronic switch within a computer that can be set to either 0 or 1. Eight bits make a *byte*. All computer data is stored in the form of bits.

Bitmap
A type of computer image in which information about the image is stored as a matrix of individual *pixels*.

BMP
A *file format*, supported by most Windows applications, for storing *bitmap* images.

Bus
A group of electrical conductors inside the computer that connects the installed devices.

Byte
A unit of information consisting of eight *bits*.

CD audio
The contents of a music compact disc.

CD-i
Compact disc interactive, a *multimedia* system from Philips. The CD-i disc is used in a CD-i player connected to a TV. CD-i discs can't be used in a *CD-ROM drive*.

CD-ROM
Compact disc read-only memory — a disc containing data that can be read by a computer but not modified. CD-ROMs can hold up to 650 *megabytes (MB)* of data and

are a popular medium for distributing *multimedia* titles.

CD-ROM drive
An item of hardware needed to read data from a *CD-ROM* and deliver the data to the PC.

CD-ROM XA
A standard for *CD-ROM*s that allows audio signals and other data (such as text and images) to be recorded on the same sector of a disc. XA stands for extended architecture.

Cel
One of a series of elements comprising a moving component in an *animation* sequence.

Channel
A pathway for transmitting messages between *MIDI sequencers* and *MIDI devices*.

Clip art
A collection of pictures, supplied on a *CD-ROM* or a floppy disk, that can be incorporated into documents or presentations.

Color depth
The number of colors that can be used for any *pixel* in a monitor display. The color depth depends on the number of bits of *video RAM* used to store the color for each pixel.

Compiler
In *multimedia*, the component of an *authoring software* package that constructs a title by interpreting commands written by the programmer.

Compression
Processing of a data file, such as a sound file, to reduce its size for storage on disk.

Controller card
See *interface card*.

CPU
Central processing unit. The component that acts as a computer's control center and the place where a program's instructions are performed.

DAC
Digital to analog conversion.

Data transfer rate
The amount of data that can be read each second from a storage medium such as a hard disk or a *CD-ROM*, usually expressed in *kilobytes (KB)* per second.

Device driver
A program that stays in memory when a PC is running and acts as a translator between the system software and a device such as a *sound card*.

Digital data
Information stored as numbers — ultimately as a sequence of 1s and 0s. The form in which all data is stored on a PC.

Digital to analog conversion
The conversion of *digital data* into an *analog signal*, such as that carried out by a *sound card* when converting a *waveform file* into a sound signal for output by speakers.

Display adapter card
A piece of hardware inside the PC that stores the images displayed on the monitor and, as it receives and assimilates signals from other parts of the computer, continuously updates the monitor display.

Display mode
The combination of the *color depth* and the *resolution* of the image displayed on the monitor screen.

Dithering
A technique for increasing the apparent number of colors in an image by using patterns of different-colored *pixels* to create blended colors.

DMA channel
Direct memory access channel. A way of transferring information directly between a device such as a *sound card* and a PC's memory.

Dot pitch
The distance between *pixels* on the monitor screen.

DPI
Dots per inch. A method of describing the *resolution* of an image for scanning or printing purposes.

Driver
See *device driver*.

e **Embedding**
The insertion of an object, such as a picture or sound file, into another file in such a way that the object is always available, even if the source file for the object is removed.

Expansion card
A piece of hardware fitted into a PC's system unit that extends the PC's capabilities — for example, a *sound card* or a *video capture* card.

Expansion connector
A slot on the PC's motherboard that provides electrical connectors for installing an *expansion card*, such as a *sound card*.

f-g **File format**
The structure of a file defining the way data in that file is stored.

FM synthesizer
A type of music *synthesizer*, used on many *sound cards*, in which sounds are produced by changing the frequency of a basic signal so that it matches the desired sound as closely as possible.

Full-motion video
Video played at a minimum of 30 frames per second.

Gray scale
The range of different shades of gray used to represent colored images.

h **Hotspot**
In a *multimedia* title, an area of the screen that, if clicked on with the mouse, causes new information to appear or the program to jump to another topic.

Hypermedia
Links between *media elements* that allow the user to browse

the information in an *interactive*, nonlinear fashion by clicking on buttons or *hotspots*. The organizational basis of many *multimedia* titles.

Hypertext
The presentation of text information as a web of connections that permits the user to browse through related topics and jump from one cross-referenced subject to another.

i-k **IDE**
Integrated drive electronics. A standard interface for hard disk drives.

Interactive
A description applied to *multimedia* titles that allow the user to control what information is displayed on screen and when it is displayed. Most interactive titles use *hypermedia* links to connect pieces of information.

Interface card
An *expansion card* added to a computer to provide an interface with an add-on piece of hardware such as a *CD-ROM drive*.

Interface connector
A connector on an *interface card* or peripheral such as a *CD-ROM drive*.

Interlaced
A type of monitor display in which the electron beams draw every other line of an image during the first pass and the lines in between on the second pass.

I/O address
A number used by a PC's *CPU* to distinguish between devices for the purposes of data transfer.

IRQ line
Interrupt request line. A pathway by which a device such as a *sound card* or *video capture* card alerts the computer's *CPU* that there is data waiting to be processed.

Jump
A shift from one topic to another in a *multimedia* title, often effected by clicking on a button or *hotspot*.

Kilobyte (KB)
Approximately 1,000 *bytes* (1,024, to be exact).

Kilohertz (kHz)
A measure of frequency. One kilohertz equals 1,000 cycles per second.

l **Land**
A level area of metal on a *CD-ROM* that represents a 0. Pits in the surface of the disc represent 1s.

Linking
The insertion of a representation of an object, such as a sound or image file, into another (destination) file. The data for the object remains in the source file. When the source file is changed, its representation in the destination file is updated.

Linear
A description applied to *multimedia* titles that limit

user involvement to advancing forward or backward one screen at a time.

 **MCI**
Media control interface.

MCI device
A device such as a *sound card* or *CD-ROM drive* that can be controlled from Windows using *media control interface* commands.

MDK
Multimedia development kit. A software package from Microsoft for programmers who want to develop *multimedia* titles for Windows.

Media control interface
A set of commands that Windows uses to control various *multimedia* devices.

Media element
Any information-containing component of a *multimedia* product — for example, text, sound, images, and video.

Media Player
A Windows utility that can be used to play *waveform files*, *MIDI files*, *animation*, and video clips.

Megabyte (MB)
Approximately one million *bytes* (1,024,000, to be exact).

MIDI
Musical instrument digital interface. A protocol that governs the exchange of data between electronic musical instruments and computers.

MIDI device
A piece of hardware that produces, handles, or interprets *MIDI* messages — for example, an electronic keyboard, a *synthesizer*, or a *MIDI interface card*.

MIDI file
A file containing instructions for a *synthesizer* to play the notes in a musical composition.

MIDI interface card
An *expansion card* that provides an interface between a PC and an external *MIDI device* (such as an external *synthesizer*).

MIDI Mapper
A Windows utility used to remap *channel* and *patch* numbers in *MIDI files* for use with particular *synthesizers*.

MIDI sequencer
A program used to record, edit, and play *MIDI files*.

Morphing
A technique for producing *animation* in which one shape or image changes into another through several intermediate stages.

MPC
A common term for a *multimedia* PC. Also the logo for the Multimedia PC Marketing Council.

Multimedia
Information presented or stored in a combination of different forms, using graphics, text, sound, video, and *animation*.

Multisession-compatible drive
A *CD-ROM drive* that can read a disc on which data has been recorded over several different sessions.

---

n **Noninterlaced**
A monitor display in which each consecutive line of an image is drawn with one pass of the electron beams.

NTSC
National Television Standards Committee — a standard used in the United States, Canada, and Japan for encoding color video signals for television broadcast and video cassette.

---

o **Object linking and embedding**
Techniques for inserting data created in one Windows application into a separate file created in the same or a different Windows application. See *embedding* and *linking*.

Object Packager
A Windows utility that can be used to insert an icon representing an object, such as an image file, into another file.

OCR
Optical character recognition.

OLE
Object linking and embedding.

Optical character recognition
The conversion of text in a scanned image file into a text file, as performed by some specialized scanning software.

---

p **PAL**
Phase Alternation Line. A standard used in Europe for encoding color video signals.

Patch
In *MIDI* terminology, a set of instrument sounds.

PCX
A common image *file format* that can handle *gray scale* and color *bitmap* images.

PhotoCD
A system developed by Kodak for storing photographs on a *CD-ROM*. Use of PhotoCD requires a *multisession-compatible drive*.

Pixel
One of the thousands of elements that make up the image displayed on the monitor screen.

Prescan
A rough image of a picture that a *scanner* displays on the monitor screen before the full scan takes place.

---

q-r **Quad-speed drive**
A *CD-ROM drive* that can transfer data at 650 *kilobytes (KB)* per second — four times faster than the drives that were first introduced.

RAM
Random access memory. Memory that is used for temporary storage of data when it is being worked on and when programs are being run.

Raster image
See *bitmap*.

Refresh frequency
The number of times per second that the image on the monitor screen is redrawn.

Resolution
The sharpness of the image on the monitor screen, determined by the number of *pixels* that make up the image.

RTF
Rich text format. A *file format* that contains not only text but also some text-formatting attributes.

Runtime engine
Software that must be distributed with a *multimedia* product in order to allow the recipient to run or use the product.

S **S-Video**
A method of splitting a video signal into two parts — the luminance (brightness and contrast) and the chrominance (hue and color saturation).

Sampling
A process carried out by a *sound card* when converting a sound wave into *digital data*, based on measuring the *amplitude* of the sound wave at small, fixed time intervals.

Sampling rate
The number of measure-ments taken per second by a *sound card* when *sampling* a sound signal, expressed in *kilohertz (kHz)*.

Scanner
A device that converts images or text into *digital data* that can be stored on a computer.

Screen capture
A technique for saving the monitor display as an image file. Captures can be performed via Windows Clipboard (by holding down Shift and pressing the Print Screen key) or by using specialized software.

SCSI
Pronounced "scuzzy." Small Computer Systems Interface. A standard type of port on an *interface card* for connecting a peripheral such as a *scanner*.

SCSI-2
An improved, faster *SCSI*.

Seek time
The time it takes a *CD-ROM drive* to move its laser beam to the part of a *CD-ROM* to be read. The shorter the seek time, the better.

Sequencer
See *MIDI sequencer*.

SIMM
Single in-line memory module. A package of memory chips mounted on one plug-in card.

Sound card
An *expansion card* that allows *waveform files* and/or *MIDI files* to be recorded and played on a PC.

Sound Recorder
A Windows utility used to record, edit, and play *waveform files*.

Streaming
The transfer of graphics, text, or audio data from a storage medium in a single, continuous stream.

SVGA
Super *VGA*. A standard for monitors in which images are displayed at a maximum *resolution* of 800-by-600 or 1024-by-768 *pixels* and a *color depth* of up to 16.77 million colors.

Synthesizer
An electronic device that can produce sounds from instructions in a *MIDI file*.

t **TIFF**
Tagged image file format. A *file format* for images, commonly used to store scanned pictures.

Tracing
A feature of *animation* software that facilitates the drawing of successive frames by displaying shadowy images of previous frames.

Transfer rate
See *data transfer rate*.

Tweening
An *animation* technique in which only certain frames in a sequence need to be drawn — the animation software works out the steps in between.

U **Vector image**
An image stored as a file that contains instructions for drawing the shapes and lines that compose the image.

VGA
Video Graphics Array. A stan-dard for monitors in which images are displayed at a maximum *resolution* of 640-by-480 *pixels* and a maximum *color depth* of 256 colors.

Video capture
The use of a special *expansion card* (a video capture card) and software to store and save a single frame, or sequence of frames, of video to disk.

Video card
See *display adapter card*.

Video driver
A *device driver* that acts as a translator between the PC's operating system and the *display adapter card*. Different drivers may be needed for different *display modes*.

Video for Windows
A set of software utilities that can be used (in conjunction with a *video capture* card) to capture a video sequence and save it with associated sound to disk, to edit a sequence, and to compress the data.

Video RAM
Memory chips on the *display adapter card* used to store all the data about the image on the monitor screen.

W **Waveform file**
A file that stores a digitized sound — for example, some spoken words, a piece of music, or a telephone's ring

WAV file
Waveform file.

DK Direct Limited would like to
thank:
Apricot Computers, UK, for loan of
a multimedia PC used to run
multimedia software and to take
screen shots featured in this book;
Corel Systems Corporation for
supplying image editing software;
Compton's New Media for
permission to use the screen from
Compton's Interactive
Encyclopedia featured on page 48
and reflected in the CD-ROM discs
featured on page 18; Dixons, UK,
for loan of the large speaker
featured on page 26;
MacWarehouse, London, UK, for
loan of the handheld scanner
featured on page 83; and Maurice
Placquet Hire Ltd. for loan of the
trumpet featured on page 7 and
the synthesizer featured on page 6
and on page 73.

All screen shots featured in this
book were taken using Collage
Complete screen capture software.

Register Today!

Return this
The Way Multimedia Works
registration card for:

✔ a Microsoft Press catalog

✔ exclusive offers on specially priced books

Fill in information below and mail postage free.

1-55615-651-0A   W9   The Way Multimedia Works

_____
NAME

_____
COMPANY

_____
ADDRESS

_____

_____
CITY   STATE   ZIP

Your feedback is important to us.

To help us make future editions even more useful, include your daytime telephone number and we might call to find out how you use *The Way Multimedia Works* . If we call you, we'll send you a **FREE GIFT** for your time!

(   )
_____
DAYTIME TELEPHONE NUMBER

The WYSIWYG Series from
Microsoft Press and Dorling Kindersley

Let the WYSIWYG (What You See Is What You Get) Series show you the easy way to learn the bestselling software available today.

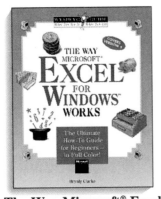 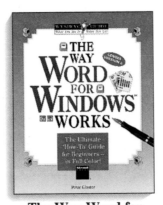 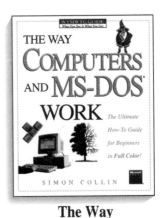

The Way Microsoft® Excel for Windows™ Works
Version 5
Brynly Clarke
$18.95   ISBN 1-55615-570-0

The Way Word for Windows™ Works
Version 6
Peter Gloster
$18.95   ISBN 1-55615-569-7

The Way Computers & MS-DOS® Work
Version 6.22
Simon Collin
$18.95   ISBN 1-55615-568-9

Microsoft Press books are available wherever quality computer books are sold. Or call 1-800-MSPRESS for ordering information. Outside the U.S., write to International Coordinator, Microsoft Press, One Microsoft Way, Redmond, WA 98052-6399.